INCREASE!

In Every Area Of Your Life

INCREASE!

In Every Area Of Your Life

DAISY S. DANIELS

THE WRITING ON THE WALL
PUBLISHING SERVICES
ORLANDO, FL 32862, U.S.A.

INCREASE! In Every Area Of Your Life
Daisy S. Daniels
P.O. Box 621433
Orlando, Florida 32862 – 1433
Website: www.thewritingonthewal.wix.com/daisysdaniels
E-Mail address: thewritingonthewall@aol.com

Library of Congress Control Number: 2015908502
ISBN 978-0-9914002-2-5

Book production by:
The Writing on the Wall Publishing Services
Cover illustration is protected by the 1976 United States Copyright Act.

Printed in the United States of America

INTRODUCTION

Like a pregnant woman in her ninth month, I have been laboring in expectation of what God is getting ready to do for His sons and daughters. This is the season that we're getting ready to birth the things of God in the earth. God is releasing blessings, breakthroughs, healings and deliverance in the earth. We are getting ready to see the manifested glory of God in our lives. We are getting ready to see the manifested miracles of God in our lives.

Don't miss this opportunity to gain insight on how to access every open door that is set before you.

Get ready to experience increase in every area of your life.

Do you want to know what God is saying? Allow me to share with you what the Lord shared with me:

> ALL OF THE PRAYERS YOU'VE PRAYED HAVE BEEN ANSWERED.
> ALL OF THE DOORS YOU WANT TO ENTER HAVE BEEN OPENED.
> YOU ARE GETTING READY TO EXPERIENCE INCREASE...IN EVERY AREA OF YOUR LIFE.
> THIS IS THE YEAR OF INCREASE!

You are getting ready to see the manifested glory of God in your life.

ALLOW GOD TO SPEAK TO YOU THROUGH HIS PROPHETIC WORD

SO YOU MAY PROSPER AND INCREASE!

"WHEN IT LOOKS LIKE NOTHING HAS HAPPENED, LOOK AGAIN. IF YOU LOOK WITH YOUR SPIRITUAL EYES, YOU'LL SEE GOD HAS GIVEN YOU INCREASE."

Some of the writings in this book were selected from *The Ties That Bind Blog* and are in their "due season." The manifestation of the word of God is being birth forth. Receive it!

To God be the glory for the things He's getting ready to do.

Daisy S. Daniels

INCREASE!

The LORD shall increase you more and more, you and your children.

Psalm 115:14 KJV

THE ROCKS

In a vision...

I saw the Lord's foot on a path of smooth stones.

Immediately, I knew the enemy was defeated, as I was reminded of the Lord crushing the head of the serpent. Then, just as suddenly, I was reminded of David with the five smooth stones, surely, the enemy is defeated!

I was reminded of a Valentine's Day gathering my husband, Randolph, and I were invited to. The stipulation for participating in this ministry of love was that we had to bring a Valentine's Day gift to exchange with one another. The gift was to be something small and creative - just for fun. Immediately, I was excited to have been invited and to take part, what girl doesn't love getting a gift? As the day drew closer, Randolph and I started to get our ideas together and prepare for the event. However, there was one problem – I could not think of anything to give him. So I called my sister, who was also invited, to see what ideas she had come up with, but still, nothing. I can't even begin to tell you how excited I was to go even though this was a very difficult time in my life. Not being able to come up with anything small, creative, and fun was adding to my frustration. Consequently, the thought crossed my mind several times to cancel. But I wanted to go. I wanted to do something fun. I wanted to be around other couples.
I was hurting.

Every idea that I came up with wasn't working. More than small, creative, and fun was my concern of not embarrassing him or myself (because the gifts would be exchanged in front of everyone.) I had to make this good.

And still, I couldn't think of anything to give him; that is, until the Holy Spirit began to minister to me.

Saddened, nervous, and almost embarrassed, "You've got to be out of your mind!" I told myself time and time again. "You've got to be kidding! There's no way you're going to do this!" I kept trying to convince myself. "But it was all that I had," I told myself as the tears started to roll down my face. And the hurt and pain began to surface. "I can't do this," I reasoned with myself. "This is not the place for that." I wiped the tears as they fell from my eyes that spoke volumes to why I had to give all that I had.

So, I gathered the gift as the Holy Spirit had instructed, and immediately my nerves went into overdrive as I tried to calm myself down during the ride to the event. We arrived at the event, but needless to say there was absolutely no way I could even enjoy myself. I was preoccupied with the gift. It was all I could think about. Oh, my God, what embarrassment; what shame I'm going to have to endure. "Please Lord," I reasoned, "this is not the place for this. It's Valentine's Day!" My mind raced as I searched the faces of the people who had come to the gathering, and could only imagine the gifts that they would give. One thing was certain, I would present last. (That probably wasn't the smartest move because the anxiety only mounted as each couple exchanged their gifts.) Oh, my God! *Just say you didn't bring a gift and just apologize to everyone,* I thought, *but what about my husband?* He'd be the only one there that wouldn't get a gift…bad idea.

And before I knew anything, we were being called up to exchange our gifts. I had already decided that he would go first. I would go last. So he started and immediately, as if all the lights had gone out, I was in the dark. And when the lights came back on...he was on one knee presenting his gift. How sweet, it was a box of chocolates! (So that should give you an idea of the types of gifts people were giving.)

Immediately, I started shaking as I tried to make light of the situation because somehow things had just gotten real. The tears began to well up in my eyes and I was doing everything I could to try to hold them back. "Oh, my God," I said. "I'm so nervous." Then the encouragement came from the crowd as someone said, "Take your time." Somehow, somebody understood what was happening. Somehow, somebody knew things had gotten serious.

Lord, please don't let me cry. I'll do it, just please don't let me cry in front of all of these people, I pleaded. Whether I cried or not, wasn't His concern. Give the gift.

So, I inhaled deeply (thinking it would stop my heart from racing – at least slow down the pace). Exhale. "Think." I encouraged myself. "You can do this." Another deep breath, then the words came out. "Sometimes in relationships there isn't always sunshine. Sometimes there's rain. Having a relationship is not always about the ups; sometimes there's hurt" (and immediately, I reached in the gift bag and handed him a rock). And with the rock in my hand, the tears again challenged me to be released as I started to choke on the words that were now caught in the lump in my throat. But I refused. And I continued. As I called out everything that I was experiencing, pain, heartache, resentment, loneliness, rejection, abandonment, which was represented by a rock, I gave the rock to him.

And with each rock that I gave him, it was that much harder to hold back the tears and the hurt, and the pain as it was all that I had to give.

He stood there with his hands held out and took them. Then all of a sudden I realized there was a silence that had fallen over the room, not a word spoken, but there were tears. Someone in the crowd understood. "Lord, help me through this," I prayed silently.
"But through it all," I continued, "we have the one rock that really matters!" And immediately, the people began to applaud as I struggled to get the words out. I reached in the bag and took out the last rock, a smooth stone, that had the name of Jesus on it, and I continued. "We have Jesus Christ, the Rock! He is the Rock Who will see us through!" And immediately, I was strengthened as the people had all began to clap and say, "Oh, my God, that was so good!"

We won the first place prize, and even to this day, when we see some of the people who were at that gathering, they never fail to mention, *the rocks.*

The interpretation of the vision...

The Lord is saying, "You've got the victory! The enemy is defeated! All you have to do is take the first step and give Him your rocks; your hurt, pain, hatred, unforgiveness, loneliness, hopelessness, bitterness, resentment, rejection that you're experiencing."

Don't be afraid. Don't be ashamed or embarrassed; give it to Jesus. The Lord is calling you to step out of your comfort zone and do something that you've never done before. While He's not asking you to attend a Valentine's Day event, He is asking you to give Him that which you hold near and dear to your heart. Yes, it may be difficult, but you've got to step out on faith. If you want to be healed, delivered, and set free, if you believe God can heal, deliver and set you free, then take that leap of faith and give Him your rocks!

INCREASE!

And in the fifth year shall ye eat of the fruit thereof, that it may yield unto you the increase thereof: I am the LORD your God.

Leviticus 19:25 KJV

LET THERE BE LIGHT!

During my morning devotion, the Lord began to minister to me, and immediately the vision was before me:

In a vision...

I saw there was light, but the earth was dark.

I was reminded of:

The earth was formless and empty, and darkness covered the deep waters. And the Spirit of God was hovering over the surface of the waters. Then God said, "Let there be light,"

Genesis 1:2-3 (NLT)

Instantly, the vision became an interpretation of us, a people, as God revealed: Somehow, someway, we've become formless and empty, as darkness covers us. And we can't seem to figure out or explain how we got here - not to ourselves or anyone else, if they asked. Lifeless, void, and in a dark place we lay before the Lord hurting and in pain. We cry out to God to deliver us; take away the hurt and the pain, do something!

Immediately I started praying that the Lord would intervene and deliver you.

It seems as though your cries go unanswered as the pain continues to go through the deepest parts of you. "Where is God?" your soul cries out as you fight back the tears that require more strength than you have, tears that require more faith than you have as you struggle with believing God would take away the pain and deliver you. But the pain has become too much for you to bear as the tears force you to continue to cry out to God, even though He doesn't answer.

And the tears roll down your face as they speak louder than any words that you could say. "Where is God?!" they scream. "Please! Take this pain away!" And yet, the darkness continues to cover those deep, dark hidden places that you swore you'd never allow to surface because they are too painful; but rather they'd stay hidden, tucked away in the emotional corners of your damaged soul. The darkness that has left you heartbroken, wounded, hurting, and suffering in silence. The darkness that keeps you from seeing God, the pain that keeps you from knowing that He's there convinces you that there's no way out.

I'm doing warfare as I bind and loose the demonic spirits that are present, and have you bound.

I have come to tell you that the Spirit of God is hovering over those deep dark places. He is watching over you. He hears every cry. He knows about every hurt and pain. The wounds of your soul lie open before Him. And He has come to deliver you!

He has come to speak to those dark places in your life; those places that have yet to be formed into that which He has created you to be. And He has come to fill those voids in your life that have left you empty – with His Holy Spirit.

To the formless, to the empty, to the darkness that covers your deepest darkest secrets; your deepest darkest hurt, your deepest darkest pain, God said, "Let there be light."

The tears began to well up in my eyes as I know your pain all too well. "Deliver them, oh, God," I plead. "Let Your light penetrate the dark places in their lives." I cried out.

And immediately after I finished praying, God said, *"...and there was light."*

Thank You, Jesus for deliverance has gone forth.

INCREASE!

*Hear therefore, O Israel, and observe to do it; that it may be well with thee, and that ye may increase mightily, as the L*ORD *God of thy fathers hath promised thee, in the land that floweth with milk and honey.*

Deuteronomy 6:3 KJV

Week 3
January 15 – January 21

MANAGE YOUR EXPECTATIONS

Often times, because of our faith in God (and what we've witnessed God do), we have great expectations of what God will do for us. And that's okay. However, our expectations are not based on understanding what God has done. They're not based on knowing how God has done what He's done. And they're not based on realizing why He has done what He's done, and yet we believe. God's going to "do it" for us.

When I say we believe God's going to "do it", I'm talking about our expectations, our thinking (or believing) that God's going to do it - and it'll just be done. For example, we want Him to deliver us out of that relationship, we have faith that He's going to do it, and we expect Him to do it - and it'll all be over. Well, that's not what God does. That's not how He does it. And that's not why He does it.

While I was in prayer, interceding on your behalf, the Lord said, "Manage your expectations."

The Lord said, "We have the wrong expectation of what, how, and why He does what He does." And therefore, we have to manage or take control of our expectations; take control of how we believe God's going to work it out. First of all, the Lord isn't going to just take you out of that relationship. That's not what He does. Second, He's not going to just stop you from being in agony. That's not how

He does it. And third, He's not going to just heal, deliver, and set you free. That's not why He does what He does.

We have unrealistic expectations of God, and His promises. Now, don't get me wrong. I do want to say that yes, there are times and situations where God does work in mysterious ways and does the impossible, but there are also times and situations where He doesn't. And this is one of those times – this is one of those situations. The Lord said, "You have to do the work." So if you want to be healed, delivered, and set free, do the work. (Or whatever it is that you want God to "do for you" – do the work.)

God is not going to just take you out of that relationship; you have to leave. You see, we're expecting God to do something and He's expecting us to do something. We're expecting Him to do "this" but He's doing "that". And just because things aren't turning out the way we expected them to turn out, doesn't mean God isn't working. It means our expectations of Him are unrealistic. He's not going to get you out, but He will enable you or strengthen you to walk away. That's what He does; that's how He works. And when you trust and depend on Him, each step of the way, that's why He does what He does.

The work is being done in you and through you – not for you.

If we don't manage our expectations of God and His promises, they will surely lead to great disappointment. And more often than not, this is why we no longer trust God to do what He said He would do; we give up, and end up staying in that relationship (because we thought He was going to just "do it" and it would've been all over with). We have unrealistic expectations that we need to manage.

[15]

While we should be focused on Him, we're focused on "it;" whatever "it" is.

If you believe God will do it, He will, but you have to be realistic, and do the work.

INCREASE!

And as soon as the commandment came abroad, the children of Israel brought in abundance the firstfruits of corn, wine, and oil, and honey, and of all the increase of the field; and the tithe of all things brought they in abundantly.

2 Chronicles 31:5 KJV

"I WILL FIGHT FOR YOU"

As the man of God ministered the word of the Lord to me, the vision of the Lord appeared before me:

In a vision...

I saw the Lord dressed in armor with a sword in His hand.

He was dressed for battle.

I couldn't help but think about what the Lord had asked me to do and how the fear of doing it was overwhelming; crippling. I was terrified, but I knew it had to be done. I struggled day in and day out. I tried time and time again to encourage myself; only to be confronted with the fear once again. The struggle was grueling as I wrestled with not only fear, but doubt, and worry as well.

However, deep inside I knew that I knew that I knew; it had to be done (no matter how difficult it may have seemed or how intimidating it was). I had to do it; even if I did it afraid.

I was reminded of the Israelites and how they spent 39 years in the wilderness unnecessarily because they were terrified of the Canaanites. (Thirty-nine years! In the wilderness! Unnecessarily! They underestimated the power of God! They underestimated God's ability!).

Often times, we're no different than the Israelites as fear grips us and keeps us from doing what God has called us to do. However, we must remember that if we are faithful to God, He will cause our opposition to disappear – in an instant!

The Lord said, "I will fight for you."

All of the time we spend struggling with fear, struggling with opposition – can be avoided if we stop underestimating the power of our God; if we stop underestimating His ability.

The interpretation of the vision…

We are being confronted by the Lord. He is commanding us to recognize His power and authority. And as we do so, He'll continue to fight for us and give us the victory. And instead of being subject to the enemy: fear, worry, doubt (or whatever opposition you may be facing), we are to be subject to Him. Our actions must line up with our confession of Christ.

The Lord is saying, as we (and I do want to stress "as" we) continue to recognize His power and authority; He'll continue to fight for us and open doors for us.

Do whatever God is telling you to do! Don't be afraid; God hasn't given us a spirit of fear, but of love, power, and a sound mind.

The Lord will fight for you!

INCREASE!

Though thy beginning was small, yet thy latter end should greatly increase.

Job 8:7 KJV

WHOSE GIFT IS IT?

There's nothing more humbling than the revelation that the gifts you've been given aren't your own; they don't belong to you. They are in fact, for someone else. And they belong to the Lord.

For many, coming to this realization will be a breakthrough.

I couldn't help but be reminded of all that I had been through; my struggles, the hurt, and pain I endured as I was wrapped up, tangled up in sin. And how desperately I wanted to get out of that situation; how desperately I wanted the pain to stop. But sadly enough, there was no one there to tell me how to get out of my situation. There was no one there that heard me crying from the excruciating pain. There was no one there to lay hands on me and cause the scales to fall from my eyes. There was no one there to prophesy to me. There was no one there to bind the spirits of hurt and pain. There was no one there to speak words of encouragement. There was no one there to give a word of knowledge or words of wisdom. There was no one there to work a miracle in my life. There was no one there to discern what I was going through. There was no one there to release the power of the Holy Spirit, so I could have a spiritual awakening.

And, it wasn't until the Lord knew that He could trust me not to go back into that situation that He saw fit to deliver me after twenty years.

The hardest lesson of all was learning that the tears, heartache, and pain were for the benefit of not only me, but for others as well; the body of Christ. That the same compassion that the Lord showed me in my time of trouble, I had to extend that same compassion as well. In my book, *The Ties That Bind*, this is what the Lord revealed:

"Every mistake that you made, God was there. Every mistake that you made, God allowed it. You are being sent to people who have made these same mistakes and you have got to tell them your story so they'll know God brought you out. You are being sent to people who want to get free."

Prophetess, Dr. Sharon D. Dominguez

You see, at some point, just like God had a plan for Jesus' life before the foundation of the world, He had a plan for us; for our life. The plan was that Christ would suffer, die on the cross, and be raised with power for us, so that we may live through Him. And the same holds true for us. Before the foundation of the world, God had a plan for us, and consequently, we also suffer, die to the flesh, and are raised with power. Not for us, but for the perfecting of the saints; the body of Christ.

We are raised with power that's demonstrated through the gifts that we've been given by the Holy Spirit who lives in us; enabling us to use the gifts.

Therefore, coming to the realization that the gifts don't belong to us, they belong to Christ; we are to use these gifts as the Lord dictates. And therefore, we don't get to pick and choose when we want to use the gifts; we use them when the Holy Spirit prompts us. We don't get to pick and choose who we want to minister to with the gifts; we use the gifts for whomever the Lord tells us. But somehow we've forgotten that.

Somehow, we've forgotten that somebody is suffering, and we have the gift they need to set them free.

Let us be mindful that the gifts were given to minister to the needs of the body of Christ for such a time as this. Let us also be mindful that if we can't be trusted to use the gifts when and with whom the Holy Spirit prompts us, the Lord will raise someone else up to carry out His plan.

Let us not forget we're the stewards of the gifts – not the owner.

And the purpose of the gifts is to help each other.

And when we get this revelation, we'll be able to build up the body of Christ.

INCREASE!

Then shall the earth yield her increase; and God, even our own God, shall bless us.

Psalm 67:6 KJV

BE PATIENT. WAIT ON GOD.

Our eyes have been opened. We see it. We want it. We understand what needs to be done to make it manifest. We've been in this place long enough; stagnant. We've missed out on the blessings before. We've missed God before. But we're determined not to let that happen again. It's time to move forward. It's time to do this thing. It's time to go to another level.

We see where we went wrong the first time, the mistakes that we made are before our eyes. Now we see the opportunities, blessings that we missed. Without a shadow of a doubt, we know what to do this time to make it right. There's absolutely no way we're going to miss God again; there's no way we're going to miss the blessings again.

We've got to fix it; we've got to get it right in order to move forward. We're anxious. We're desperate. We've suffered long enough. We have to make it right!

Let me encourage you today: Be patient. Wait on the Lord.

It's the right thing to do, but it's the wrong time.

We have to be careful that in our attempt to make it right; in our attempt of not missing the next opportunity – the next blessing, that we don't get ahead of God.

Do only what He's telling you to do; not what you know needs to happen.

In our desperate attempt to right the wrong, we move outside of the will of God; which results in us doing things in our own strength. And consequently, every attempt fails. Our efforts are fruitless. And there will be road block after road block. Frustration, spirit disturbed, and disappointed.

We lose faith in God.

How can this be? (We know it's the right thing to do.)

It's the wrong time.

Be patient. Wait on the Lord.

We've suffered, been stagnant, and now we desperately want to move forward from this place. We've got to do something!

Yes, we can do something.

"Be patient. Wait on the Lord."

Wait. It is the catalyst of all that the Lord has planned for us.

Let's not get ahead of Him.

Let's focus on the doors that He has opened and not on the ones that we want opened.

Be patient. It allows Him to work it out for us. He knows the road blocks that are ahead.

Be patient. He knows the obstacles that we're going to face. And He's preparing us.

Wait on the Lord.

But they that wait upon the Lord shall renew their strength; they shall mount up with wings as eagles; they shall run, and not be weary; and they shall walk, and not faint.

Isaiah 40:31 KJV

Waiting on the Lord is having the patient expectation that God will fulfill His promises and strengthen us to rise above the difficulties.

Wait on the Lord and be confident that His purposes will be accomplished.

Be patient as the Lord makes spiritual progress within us with spiritual power.

Be patient as we come to the realization that the spiritual harvest is more important than the natural blessing.

Let Him have His way. That way, we will be effective. That way, we'll receive what God has for us. And that way God will get the glory!

Otherwise, we'll faint, and not receive the promise.

INCREASE!

A man's belly shall be satisfied with the fruit of his mouth; and with the increase of his lips shall he be filled.

Proverbs 18:20 KJV

Week 7
February 12 – February 18

BUILD AN ARK

In a vision...

I saw Noah building the ark.

The interpretation of the vision...

The Lord said, "We have to be diligent, work day and night; without ceasing – until the promise comes."

There are many of you who are expecting God to do something for you; heal, deliver, and set you free. And just like Noah, God is saying that He wants a long-term commitment from you, to do for you what you want Him to do. Therefore, we must take a page from Noah's notebook: Noah was faithful, obedient, he believed God, and did exactly as God commanded him to do - then he was saved; delivered from the impending flood upon the earth.

There are several things that we must take note of when it comes to the promises of God:

- ✓ He was very specific about what He was going to do.
- ✓ He was very specific about why He was going to do it.
- ✓ He was very specific about when the flood would come.
- ✓ He was very specific about how long it would last.

[29]

- ✓ He was very specific about His instructions to build the ark. And...
- ✓ He was very specific about who was to enter in.

We serve a God who is concerned about every detail, the specifics, and every aspect of our lives. He is in the details. Therefore, your deliverance is going to require obedience unto Him, which means you'll have to commit long-term so that deliverance will come forth in your life.

Deliverance is not about a quick, easy, and/or painless fix. It's about God keeping your feet from stumbling so that you may be able to walk upright before Him. It's about allowing Him to have His way with you and doing in you what He wants to do. It's about getting you to a place in Him that will accomplish His purpose in the earth.

"Come to me. Trust me," says the Lord. So if you want God to heal, deliver, and set you free, seek His face. It's going to require you to be patient and wait on the Lord. God's promise is to those who wait on Him, trust in Him, and His timing. His timing is perfect. Everything you need is in Him; He has already made a way for you; you've got the victory!

Like Noah, the first thing you've got to do is start building. He started preparing for that which God promised; deliverance by being obedient to the Lord's commands. Obedience is preparation for the blessings. Be diligent, work day and night; without ceasing – until the promise comes." Remove yourself from that situation, relationship, and/or environment. And meditate on the Word of God day and night. Immerse yourself in His presence. And He'll do just what He said He'll do.

The scripture tells us that Noah did everything as the LORD commanded him.

Will you?

INCREASE!

A wise man will hear, and will increase learning; and a man of understanding shall attain unto wise counsels:

Proverbs 1:5 KJV

Week 8
February 19 – February 25

GOD IS OPENING DOORS

As I lie in bed, I was startled by the loud knock on the door. I jumped up; my heart raced, but quickly calmed down as I reasoned that it must be my son. "Come in," I said. But there was no answer. "Come in," I said louder, but still there was no answer. As I lie in bed, I suddenly realized the angel of the Lord had knocked on the door. I had overslept. I hadn't gotten up for my morning devotion, and was satisfied with just giving in to the defeat that was beckoning me to give up as the tears rolled down my face.

The next morning, as I lie in bed, again, I was startled by the loud knock on the door. Again, I jumped up; my heart raced, but without any thought I said, "Come in." But again, there was no answer. "Come in," I said louder for a second time, but still there was no answer. I comforted myself as I looked around; I know I heard a knock. The next thing I knew, the door opened as my husband asked, "What are you saying?"

"Did you knock on the door?" I asked.

"No. No one knocked on the door," he responded.

"I heard a knock on the door."

"There wasn't a knock on the door," he assured me, "I'm the only one here, and I didn't knock on the door."

Again, I realized the knock on the door had come from heaven. Again, I had overslept. For the second day, I hadn't gotten up for devotion and was still struggling with just giving up as all of my inadequacies surfaced. I was tired and was about to succumb to the thought that nothing was happening; in spite of all the efforts I'd put forth.

That night, as soon as I laid down, I don't even think my head hit the pillow, and there was a knock on the door. I jumped up, and asked my husband, "Did you hear that?!"

"Hear what?"

"The knock on the door; there was a knock on the door. You didn't hear that?"

"No."

"There *was* a knock," I said to convey *I know I heard a knock.*

The Lord had come for a visitation. He wanted to talk, and He wanted my attention.

While I was in devotion, immediately the vision was before me:

I saw the Lord's foot push open a door.

The vision appeared before me three times. And immediately the Lord began to minister to me:

Suddenly, I knew I had the victory and the Lord was opening a door for me. *Opening doors* rung out in my spirit. Not just *a door,* but *doors; many doors* are being opened as the three visions confirmed. And therefore, I want to share with you what the Lord shared with me:

Sadly we've missed out on the blessings of the Lord because *we've failed to recognize* the "knock on the door." We have missed out on the blessings of the Lord because *we've failed to answer* the "door of opportunity." Because somehow, someway, we've come to understand that when God opens a door, THAT'S IT! *That's the blessing!*

What we don't understand is the knock at the door opens a pathway in which we are to go; the direction in which we must go, in order to "get to" the blessing. That's why often times, when we do answer the door, it's not the blessing we were expecting, so we close the door and walk away from the blessing.

We want the blessing, but we don't want to do the work to get to the blessing.

We must also understand that in order for us to receive the blessings of God, we have to be prepared for them; there is a process we have to go through to not only be ready for *it*, but for *it* to be ready for *us!* Blessings don't just happen overnight – it's a process.

Do we understand?

When God opens a door, He is giving us an opportunity to do something that we weren't able to do on our own – that's a blessing!

When God opens a door, He is giving us an opportunity to go somewhere that we weren't able to go on our own – that's a blessing!

When God opens a door, He is giving us an opportunity to act in *His* timing. And that's a blessing!

And the vision that was before me confirmed the word of the Lord; we have the victory and God is opening doors for us.

This is not the time for feeling defeated. This is not the time to lie down and cry. This is not the time for sleeping late. This is not the time to give up.

NOW is the time to answer the knock at the door because your blessing is on the other side! That thing you've been asking God to do for you – is happening right now. God is doing it; He's making a way for you!

When you are doing what God has called you to do, "opportunity" comes looking for you! And it won't stop knocking until you open the door. The blessings will come up from behind and overtake you.

And suddenly, as I continued to sit before the Lord, I felt an urgency in my spirit. "Make haste," says the Lord. Just like the children of Israel leaving Egypt, *God is moving*. NOW is the time! Do it now while the doors are open! Whatever it is that God has called you to do, "Do it now!" says the Lord.

INCREASE!

The meek also shall increase their joy in the LORD, and the poor among men shall rejoice in the Holy One of Israel.

Isaiah 29:19 KJV

"DO IT NOW!"

As the Lord continues to encourage me, I can hardly contain the excitement of what He's doing.

The word of the Lord has been confirmed:

God Is Opening Doors.

He is opening doors for us that are enabling us to do what we've never done; to go where we've never been. And while we may be excited to hear that God is doing something; moving on our behalf, we understand that when God opens a door no man can shut it; however, we must also understand that *God* will shut the door when the time is up (ask Noah). And when the door shuts, no man can open it!

We have let fear hold us back, and it's keeping us from doing what we've been called to do. But the Lord says, "Do not fear. I am with you. I will lead and guide you." Yes, it may be frightening, but we've got to do it anyway. We're doing something that we've never done; we're going where we've never been. But we've got to encourage ourselves in the Lord that He would enable us to do that which the enemy is trying to stop us from doing. We must recognize that "fear" is the enemy's tactic to keep us from doing what God called us to do. He's trying to stop us from getting the blessings that God has promised.

That's why we must "make haste," says the Lord. We can't wait to do it; we've got to do it now while the opportunity is available to us; while the door is open.

"Do it with urgency!" says the Lord.

Now is not the time to fall back; shrink back. Now is not the time to give up; get tired. Now is not the time to haphazardly do it; do it with urgency!

What has the Lord instructed you to do? Whatever it is, do it! "Do it now!" says the Lord. Doing it and doing it now is a sign of our faith; that God is going to do just what He said He'd do. Doing it and doing it now is us getting prepared for the blessing. Our preparation is an act of faith; preparing ourselves for the fulfillment of God's promise.

Don't let it be said, "Too late."

He who has an ear let him hear what the Spirit is saying to the church.

INCREASE!

And I will gather the remnant of my flock out of all countries whither I have driven them, and will bring them again to their folds; and they shall be fruitful and increase.

Jeremiah 23:3 KJV

THIS IS NOT LOVE

Recently I was asked about my book *The Ties That Bind.* I shared that it's about my testimony of brokenness and how among my many struggles, I had suffered physical abuse at the hands of my then intimate partner. "In fact," I said, "I share the intimate details of not only the physical, but emotional and psychological abuse as well."

Therefore, please allow me to preface this by saying that while we are on the heels of the Ray Rice and then fiancé, Janay Palmer's story; of him knocking her unconscious on the elevator. This isn't just about Ray Rice and Janay Palmer.

Many of us have expressed our opinions of what should and shouldn't be done regarding Rice's career, his punishment; him being held accountable for his actions. And many of us have also expressed our opinions of whether or not Janay should've married him, if she should've stayed, and/or why did she stay. And yet, we've failed to take the plank out of our own eye.

Again, I want to say, this incident really isn't just about Ray Rice or Janay Palmer; this is about us.

This is a wakeup call. Do you hear the alarm going off?

You see, while many of us are able to say what we would and wouldn't do, what we would and wouldn't take, and if

I were him or if I were her, the truth of the matter is, most of us are enduring that same abuse just on a different level. The abuse may not have escalated to us being knocked unconscious physically, but we've been knocked unconscious emotionally, psychologically, and I'll even go as far as to say, spiritually.

In fact, some of us are still unconscious.

I understand. He never slapped, pushed, shoved, or abused you physically in the slightest way, okay. But what about the emotional and psychological abuse you suffer as a result of his infidelity; the relationships that he's had (and continues to have) with other women, and you stay? Okay, so you think, as long as he's coming home that you're not affected. Don't be fooled. You are being affected; you are being abused emotionally and psychologically as you continue to try to hold on to him and tolerate this type of behavior.

The alarm is sounding.

You are in an abusive relationship.

It's time for us to wake up – and respond.

I understand. We don't know it's physical abuse because it's just a push and that was the first time it happened. We don't know that it's abuse because it's just a slap in the face. We don't see it as abuse because in our minds physical abuse is when you are being beaten severely. If it's not a black eye, broken arm or bruised body, then it's not abuse.

I understand. We don't realize we're being abused because he said it was just sex, she didn't mean anything to him.

We don't realize we're being abused because he said he was sorry every time it happened. We don't see it as abuse because in our minds we are convinced he loves us. If he didn't, he wouldn't be with me.

And consequently, before we realize it, we're in so deep that there's no way out. And as the abuse escalates, we continue to go back and forth with the desire to leave that's overruled by the love (and fear) that makes us stay.

The alarm is sounding.

I understand. What they see from the outside looking in is not what we see on the inside looking out.

We don't see what they see. We can't hear the alarm going off. We're unconscious. We cannot respond.

I understand. Yes, I stayed. Why? I wanted to stay. Why? I loved him.

But let me make this clear: I didn't write this to ask, "Why don't you leave?" I didn't write this to say, "When you get tired of the abuse, you'll leave."

But I did write this to say, "This is not love."

God wants to heal, deliver, and set you free from *The Ties That Bind.* As long as you are unconscious and not responding spiritually, you cannot receive the love, healing, or blessings of God. God would not have you to suffer in an abusive relationship, but rather He wants to awaken your consciousness.

INCREASE!

And I will multiply upon you man and beast; and they shall increase and bring fruit: and I will settle you after your old estates, and will do better unto you than at your beginnings: and ye shall know that I am the LORD.

Ezekiel 36:11 KJV

HE WANTS MORE

In a dream...

I was "on my way" – doing what the Lord had instructed me to do. I got right to the door and somehow, seemingly, I was just standing there – I was distracted. However, I noticed the person I passed on the way had now gone in the door and the door closed.

Immediately, I was overcome with great disappointment as I said to myself, *I was just standing here! I was right here!* In disbelief that I was so close and missed the opportunity to go in. How could I be so close and not go in? I had to go in!

I started to bang on the door.

Now I did notice that while the door had been closed, it wasn't closed all the way; it wasn't locked. I could see that if I pushed the door it would probably open. But I kept banging on the door as if to say, "I was right here! Let me in!"

The man opened the door and I went in.

However, once inside, to my surprise, there were only a few people. And I was concerned.

Then I woke up.

My immediate thought was that I had "almost" missed an opportunity. While I was standing right at the door, somehow, I had let the door close before I got the chance to go in because I had gotten distracted. Now while I do want to say, "Don't get distracted," that's not the message the Lord is conveying.

I couldn't help but contemplate the door seemingly being closed and then opened.

Well, I knew right away that it wasn't God – because the door He opens, no man can close and the door He closes no man can open! So I knew it wasn't God who had opened or closed the door, it was man.

Again, while I will say, "walk through the doors that God has open for us, not man," that's not the message the Lord is conveying either.

As I inquired of the Lord concerning the interpretation of the dream, the Lord said, "To whom much is given, much is required." And immediately, He began to say that the door that we're trying to go through; that thing that we're trying to do is too small; it's not enough. The people are too few and the platform is too small. He wants us to do more. We should be using a larger platform to reach more of His people. However, we're not doing enough with the resources, talents, and gifts that He has given us, and we're not using them effectively.

The open doors that God has for us are on larger platforms to reach more of His people.

My God! God is doing a new thing; on a higher level.

Let's pursue the doors that He has open for us.

And as we pursue these platforms, He will give us more opportunities. (And if we're given more opportunities, we'll also be given more responsibility.) And the Lord is holding us accountable for using that which He has given us effectively. We've been entrusted with much, and even more is required.

God has opened doors to larger platforms to reach more of His people – to do His will.

Focus on the areas in your life where you believe God is asking for more.

INCREASE!

And the apostles said unto the Lord, Increase our faith.

Luke 17:5 KJV

HE'S NOT YOUR HUSBAND

As I lie before the Lord, I was reminded of The Woman At The Well in John, chapter four. In particular, I was reminded of Jesus saying to her, "Go and get your husband."

"I don't have a husband," the woman replied.

Jesus said, "You're right! You don't have a husband – for you have had five husbands, and you aren't even married to the man you're living with now. You certainly spoke the truth!"

I couldn't help but be reminded of my own deepest, darkest secrets; my own deepest darkest pain that I shared in *The Ties That Bind.* Just as He did with the woman at the well, the Lord had come to get to the root of why I had found myself at the well. A place that was supposed to be a source of abundant supply had become a dry place – my well had run dry.

His presence made known that it was time to face the facts.

As I continued to cry out to the Lord, I tried desperately to draw from Him, to get from Him what I needed; that which would get me through this difficult time. I sat before the Lord and then I heard in my spirit, "Give Me whatever it is that you came here for."

Immediately, I knew the Lord was asking me to do something that I wasn't willing to do.

"What do I have to give?" I cried out. "I'm coming to You for help, Lord. You've got to help me through this. I don't know what to do. I can't take it anymore. Please, Lord. Help me."

"Give it to me," He said.

"What is it? What do you want? Whatever it is, Lord, take it." I said. Then I realized that the Lord was telling me to give Him my hurt and pain. Give Him everything that I had been holding on to for so long. Everything that I had been through in my relationship – give it to Him.

However, I became overwhelmed at the thought of relinquishing, giving up or losing out – after all that I had been through. And therefore, I wanted nothing to do with what Jesus was commanding me to do. So I cried out, "How can You ask me to give You what has been the only thing that I live for? I've come a long way; it took many years to get this far. How can You ask me to give it to You?"

"If you knew the gift that I have for you; if you knew that I will give you life, you will never have to thirst again – you will never have to experience that hurt and pain again. Come into My presence and ask Me to deliver you from the hurt, pain, anger, and fear. Ask Me to renew your mind, so that you aren't tormented with the thoughts. Ask Me to draw you closer to Me – and give you the strength to walk away. Ask Me to pour into you if you have a revelation of Who I AM."

"Lord, You have nothing to draw with," I reasoned, "obviously, You have no idea how much pain I have had to experience or you wouldn't be asking me to do this. You have no idea of the hurt that I have had to endure or how long I have had to suffer in order to just get to the well. You have no idea of how difficult it had been to draw from You or how far I have had to come. Besides, this well is deep. The hurt and the pain go deeper than even *I* had imagined. You have nothing that can reach down deep enough, far enough to get to the bottom of what I have in this heart of mine – called a well. So, don't ask me to draw *for* you."

As the tears rolled down my face, I could feel the pain began to surface. I didn't want to deal with it. I didn't want to face the hurt and the reality that something was wrong. This wasn't how it was supposed to be.

The man I was intimate with was not my husband. The man I so desperately wanted; the man I would (and had) done any and everything possible for, the man I desperately tried to hold on to...was not my husband. He was not the man that God had for me.

After all that I had been through with this man.

You see, we hurt because we're trying to hold on to something that God has said we cannot have. And the longer we hold on to it, the more hurt and pain we'll endure. There's only one way to stop the hurt and pain. There's only one way to stop the tears from falling from your eyes. And that is, to come to the realization that he's not your husband. He's not who God has for you.

God is not going to bless something that He didn't establish.

Of course it's going to be difficult to let go. Of course it's going to be hard to move on. But it's going to more difficult, and even harder the longer you stay.

The well has run dry.

Draw from the well that fills the heart with the joy of the Lord. Give it to Jesus. Let him go.

INCREASE!

He must increase, but I must decrease.

John 3:30 KJV

DO WHAT HE SAYS. FOLLOW HIM.

I was awakened, but not startled by the knock on the door. I knew the angel of the Lord was at the door. I got up and went into the Lord's presence to see what He was saying; why had He come?

As the Lord ministered to me, He reminded me of the angel that came to free Peter from prison (as Peter slept) in Acts, chapter twelve. The angel woke Peter up and commanded him to get up, get dressed, and follow him. He then led Peter to the city gate, which we're told opened for them all by itself.

I began to realize that like Peter, we've probably found ourselves in a place where we may feel stuck, a place where we may feel restricted, a place where we feel we should be doing more; especially since we're doing what the Lord told us to do. And we wonder, even question, how did we end up here – in this place?

While we may think we have some valid reasons for feeling this way, let me ask you this: Is it possible that like Peter you aren't aware that you are walking in that which you have prayed for? Do you realize that the thing you asked for, prayed for is actually happening? Have you lost focus of what it is that you're doing and why you're in the place that you're in?

Like Peter, all we have to do is: Do what He's telling us to do and follow Him. And like Peter, He will lead us to the place where we should be. He will lead us to the place where we're most effective; the place where we will have the greatest impact. And just as He did for Peter, He will lead us from a place of confinement to the gate that leads to the city; that leads to the people that He has ordained to receive us.

Could it be that we can't see what the Lord is doing because we're not walking by faith, which has caused us to lose hope? Have we become discouraged, disappointed because what we see doesn't look like what we've been praying for? If we open our eyes and walk by faith, we'll see that we're walking in the manifested blessings of God. We'll see that we're doing exactly what we've been praying for; God has answered our prayers!

Is it possible that we're so focused on doing what we want to do, and going where we want to go, that we can't comprehend what God is doing? The things we're trying to do and the places we're trying to go are too small for what God wants to do through us.

We're thinking too small.

What God is getting ready to do in our lives will far exceed our expectations; anything that we could even think or imagine, if we just do what He's telling us to do, and follow Him.

Jesus is trying to take us from "doors of opportunities" to "gates that lead to the city"!

The things that we're doing now (though they seem insignificant) are going to be the very things that will open the gate and lead us to the city. And I can't say it enough: "What God has for us is so much more than what we could ever think or imagine."

But instead of following Jesus, and keeping our eyes on Him, we have become like Rhoda (and the others who were praying); we don't believe that the thing that we've been praying for is here! How could we not believe that the knock on the door is what we've prayed for? How could we not believe that He would do just what He said He would do?

If we would just stay focused on what it is that the Lord has called us to do, if we'll just manage our expectations of what we think the blessing should look like, we'll see that the thing we've been praying for is at the door; the Lord has given us what we've asked for.

All we have to do is: Do what He says, follow Him, and He will lead us to the place where He would have us; the place with the greatest impact!

Do you want "doors of opportunity" or "gates that lead to the city"? Do you want the Lord to lead you to more blessings; bigger blessings?

Then we must be mindful that the things we're doing now are going to cause the gate to open by itself, if we continue to be obedient to what He's telling us to do.

And like Peter, we need to come to our senses and realize this thing is really happening!

INCREASE!

I have planted, Apollos watered; but God gave the increase.

1 Corinthians 3:6 KJV

SEED TO THE SOWER

There was a knock on the door. I wasn't expecting anyone so when I heard the knock I was surprised. The knock was loud and almost thunderous. The knock came with such authority; demanding that the door be opened.

To my surprise it was a box addressed to me. When I opened the box and saw the package inside, I had no idea of what to expect. My initial thought was *I hope the Lord was sending me some encouragement.* When I opened the package, immediately I got excited.

It was an unexpected blessing!

Unexpected because I had been spending so much of my time focused on the one thing that God was doing in my life. So when the package came, it was a clear indication that God had not only sent me some encouragement, but He had kept His promise.

It was almost as if the Lord was reminding me or assuring me that while it may have seemed that things weren't moving as fast as I would've liked them to move or things weren't happening the way that I would've liked for them to happen, He was working things out on my behalf.

Although there were many days that I struggled and had to encourage myself, the knock on the door was a reminder that He hadn't forgotten about me. And I could rest assured that He would do just what He said He would do.

As the Lord ministered to me, He reminded me of:

For God is the one who provides seed for the farmer and then bread to eat. In the same way, He will provide and increase your resources and then produce a great harvest of generosity in you.
2 Corinthians 9:10 NLT

Immediately, I couldn't help but be reminded of how often we miss the blessings of God because we don't see the blessings that God has for us; because they don't look like what we think they should look like. And I can't say it enough; we have to continue to walk by faith and not by sight. We want to be careful that we are not rejecting the blessings of God because they don't look like what we thought they should look like.

What we've failed to realize is that the blessings of God are seeds.

He intentionally gives us seeds because it is our responsibility to produce a harvest.
I'm sure we've heard of the analogy of the oak tree. While it is one of the biggest and strongest trees there are, it doesn't start out as an oak tree – it starts out as a seed.
It becomes our responsibility to plant, water (develop) the seed that He gives us then God will give the increase. He'll give you even more as you cultivate and develop what He's given you. That's the blessing!

The blessing is in the seed!

This is why we miss God's blessings: We're looking for an oak tree, when God has given us the seed - inside the seed is the oak tree. Inside the seed is your blessing. The thing you've been praying for! Do you know what your seed, your blessing looks like?

He gives the seed to the person who can work the field. If He didn't think you could produce a harvest, He wouldn't give you the seed.

What are you going to do with the seed God has given you?

INCREASE!

Now he that ministereth seed to the sower both minister bread for your food, and multiply your seed sown, and increase the fruits of your righteousness;

2 Corinthians 9:10 KJV

BE RESTORED

As the Lord ministered to me, *restored* was prompted in my spirit. And immediately, I knew I was being restored. I couldn't help but think about the years that I suffered; the hurt and pain that I endured. All those years, lost. Somehow, everything that I had was, lost. Everything that I was, lost. Nothing left! All was broken – heart, mind, body and soul. All was lost – dreams, goals, and aspirations. The enemy had taken everything that I had. I had nothing left to give.

And just as suddenly, I was reminded of how the Lord restored me as my healing and deliverance came forth. Restoration; as He made me whole again.

And even now, as I see the Lord opening doors for me, there is no mistaking - He's giving me back everything that the enemy stole from me. He's giving it all back – dreams, goals, and aspirations. He's establishing me in my rightful place; giving me favor with God and with man (in the Kingdom and in the natural).

As He opens doors, establishes businesses, and declares His word.

How the years seemed to have been lost – the excitement, the hunger, the thirst, the desire – gone; seemingly dead.

And yet, every now and again, something happened, something was said that would spark a little flicker of hope that declared, "It's going to happen! God's going to do it!"

The years were long and painful.

As we waited, as we suffered, we were bowed down; couldn't see our way – couldn't see no way. We didn't think it would ever happen - didn't know if it would ever happen. How desperately we didn't want that to be the case.

God had to do it! He said He would. And we know that He's not a man that He should lie.

It was hard to wait and keep waiting. It was hard to trust and keep trusting. It was hard to believe and keep believing. It was hard to hope and keep hoping. It was hard to dream and keep dreaming.

It was hard to have faith.

But somehow, in the midst of all the hurt, pain, disappointment, discouragement; in the midst of the doubt, worry, and confusion; in the midst of the heaviness, the burden that weighed on us – there was God.

It didn't matter how long it would take; it didn't matter how far we had to go; it didn't matter when it would happen, but now, when we look back, we see the steps that we took to get here (although there weren't many). We see the work that we did (although it wasn't much). We see the light of hope that would not go out (although it was only a flicker).

Somewhere in our heart of hearts, somehow in the midst of the storm, we believed.

And as the tears rolled down our faces we knew that they would be the witness to all that was buried under the hurt, pain, disappointment that tried desperately to make us give up...but we refused!

We stood on His word. We stood on His promise. We waited on Him.

Though it was long and hard, we waited.

And now, God is restoring us.

And I will restore to you the years that the locust hath eaten, the cankerworm, and the caterpillar, and the palmerworm, my great army which I sent among you.

Joel 2:25 KJV

All that was lost is now found.

All that was stolen is now being returned.

All that was devoured is now being replaced.

Everything that the enemy stole from you!

He's giving it back!

Now be restored!

INCREASE!

From whom the whole body fitly joined together and compacted by that which every joint supplieth, according to the effectual working in the measure of every part, maketh increase of the body unto the edifying of itself in love.

Ephesians 4:16 KJV

PREGNANT IN THE SPIRIT

All of a sudden, I was craving popcorn. Popcorn had become my "go-to" snack. And not the fit, healthy stuff I might add; the more butter, the better. I went from a discipline of no snacks to eating popcorn every day. I mean, I couldn't finish my dinner before I was reaching for the popcorn. (And to be honest, some days, I started with the popcorn before I ate dinner). Then I noticed I was "getting out of control," and became disturbed in my spirit.

And my prayer for the night became, "Lord, reveal to me what's going on."

In a dream…

The Lord revealed to me that I am pregnant; in the spirit.

As the Lord ministered to me, He reminded me of Hannah, in 1 Samuel, chapter 1. Now some of you may know about Hannah; how she desperately wanted a baby, but the Lord had closed up her womb. She had not been able to conceive. She was so desperate; in fact, she stopped eating, and was in deep anguish as she cried out to God bitterly.

Now, what we may not realize when something like this happens is we're trying to feed in the natural what we're craving in the spirit. Well, let me say it this way; we're trying to deal with what's going on in the spirit with natural responses. You see, often times, when we find ourselves in situations where we may feel inadequate, inferior, or even overwhelmed, we use whatever coping mechanism we can to help us deal with the stress of it all.

Basically, Hannah was responding in the natural to what God was doing in the spirit.

However, what she failed to realize (or didn't know) was God had closed up her womb because He was preparing her for the birthing of Samuel. (Not eating, in deep anguish, crying bitterly unto the Lord was her way of dealing with the stress of it all; it was her way of coping with a spiritual issue in the natural.)

She wanted desperately what only God could do.

So, in essence, being pregnant in the spirit means:

- ✓ God is birthing something in you.
- ✓ God is developing you (preparing you) for whatever it is that He's getting ready to bring forth in your life.
- ✓ You're getting ready to go through a developmental stage; the birthing process – as He prepares you for the promise He has for you.

In other words, you're experiencing some growing pains; feeling a little discomfort, uncomfortable if you will, in a place you've never been in before, doing things you've never done before. That's why you're craving in the natural what's going on in the spirit – this is your way of coping with what God is doing in your life.

It may not be "popcorn" or "not eating at all," but you have a way of coping with what God is doing in your life.

Now, like Hannah, we have to be careful with how we manage the discomfort of carrying the weight of this pregnancy; we have to be careful wiith how we manage the weight of the promise.

Like Hannah, we have to pray. We have to let prayer become our "go-to" way of responding to what God is doing in our lives. We have to stay in His face, and allow Him to complete the work in us.

God is the only one who can prepare us; develop us - get us ready for the promise.

And like Hannah, in due season, God will birth forth His promise in us.

INCREASE!

And not holding the Head, from which all the body by joints and bands having nourishment ministered, and knit together, increaseth with the increase of God.

Colossians 2:19 KJV

WHAT ARE YOU AFRAID OF?

I worked so hard and so long only to run into a road block.

But I've worked long enough to know that road blocks won't stop me. I'm determined and whatever I have to do, I'm going to get it done. All I need is a little encouragement; to step away, take a deep breath, then go back to it later, when I'm no longer frustrated.

But something happened during the night.

There would be no going back to it in the morning. Because the Lord revealed to me that the road block would not be removed. It was there for a reason. And it had nothing to do with trying harder, staying the course, or not giving up.

The road block was there to lead me back to what it was that I was *supposed* to be doing.

You see, I was doing what I wanted to do; what I was comfortable with. But I wasn't doing what the Lord told me to do.

I had gotten side tracked.

My fear, anxiety, and inadequacy had diverted me from what I was supposed to be doing, to doing what I was comfortable with (and good at).

And yet, they had taken me off course.

And instead of me following Jesus, I was telling Him to follow me: Look, I'm good at what I do. There's no anxiety, fear, or lack. Everything I need to get the job done – I have. I have the skills. I have the knowledge. I have resources. And there isn't a challenge that I can't overcome – I got this!

But what are we really accomplishing if it's outside of the will of God? If it's not what He told us to do, what are we really accomplishing?

Nothing!

Time wasted. Skills wasted! Resources wasted! Efforts wasted!

Destiny delayed.

You see, it's like Paul said, we do the things we're not supposed to do, and the things that we're supposed to do…we don't do.

Of course it's difficult to do things that we're not familiar with; things that challenge us, and causes us to come face to face with our fear, anxiety, and shortcomings. Of course we're going to be afraid. Of course there's going to be "what ifs." And of course there's going to be some mistakes.

But it's all a part of the developmental stage. It's all a part of God developing us to get us to the place where He wants us to be.

Follow Him.

God is in control.

He's the one who develops the gift; perfects the gift. He determines what we do with the gift (if it's going to be effective).

The thing He's telling us to do will challenge us in areas where God will get the glory; not us. The thing He's telling us to do will result in us having to trust Him to get it done. The thing He's telling us to do will highlight our lack of confidence because we're not self-sufficient. The thing He's telling us to do will constantly question *how is this going to happen?*

It'll require us to do something that we've never done before, and cannot do on our own.

That way, only God gets the glory.

What are you afraid of?

What did God tell you to do (that you're not doing)?

The roadblock is not going to be removed.

God will get the glory out of every fear; every inadequacy and every mistake.

The very thing that we fear is going to be the very thing that God will use to thrust us to the next level.

INCREASE!

And the Lord make you to increase and abound in love one toward another, and toward all men, even as we do toward you:

1 Thessalonians 3:12 KJV

HE WON'T LET YOU FALL

In a dream…

I was sitting on the edge.

Now I must say that I was surprised at how relaxed I was. In fact, I wasn't bothered at all by the situation, which was surprising to me. There have been many times when I was "standing" on the edge and was terrified. Not because I wanted to jump, but because I was afraid to jump – you know, taking that next step! Because I didn't see any way that I would make it.

It was frightening!

But this time, it wasn't and, I wasn't. I was just sitting there.

Then all of a sudden, I slipped off.

And somehow (don't ask me how because it was the grace of God), I managed to grab hold of the edge with one hand as I cried out to Jesus to help me. (If I fell, my life would've been over).

And instantly, He caught me and lifted me back up onto the edge.

Well, once again, He saved me.

Once again, He has proven Himself!

So many times I've been on the ledge or "on the verge" of doing something, "on the verge" of getting the blessing, and it was terrifying to take that next step.

And I'm sure many of you may have found yourselves in that same situation: afraid to take the next step, afraid that you may fall (or fail) while so close to the blessing.

The interpretation of the dream…

Jesus is not going to let you fall.

He won't let you fail. He's right there waiting to catch you – if you call out to Him.

I know you're thinking how devastating it would be if you fail because there would be no way that you'd be able to recover:

This is the very thing that you've dreamed of.
This is the very thing that you've worked so hard and so long for.
This is the very thing that you quit your job for.

This is it!

But what would be even more devastating is if you were on the edge of getting that blessing and was too afraid to take the next step. And even more devastating is if you did fall and your trust wasn't in Jesus (but rather in your own strength and abilities). And even more devastating is if you did fall, and "He" doesn't save you.

Put your trust in Jesus.

He won't let you fall.

Everything that you've been praying for, believing for, hoping for is right there.

You are right on the verge of getting your breakthrough.

Trust Him.

How many times have we gotten right to the door of the blessing and didn't go in (because we were afraid)? How many times have we been "on the verge" of getting the blessings and missed the opportunity (because we were afraid)?

Don't be afraid.

Take the next step.

He is waiting to catch you, if you fall.

My sisters and brothers, you can't fail with Jesus!

The thing you're doing – it's not going to fail.

You will receive the blessings of the Lord!

INCREASE!

And indeed ye do it toward all the brethren which are in all Macedonia: but we beseech you, brethren, that ye increase more and more;

1 Thessalonians 4:10 KJV

YOU ARE ON THE VERGE OF A BREAKTHROUGH!

I was desperate. I needed a word from the Lord. I needed a breakthrough.

There was something going on in the spirit, but I didn't know what. I felt like I couldn't push forward. I couldn't take another step. I couldn't pray another prayer; I had prayed all I could pray. I had done all that I could do. I had stood for as long as I could stand. There was nothing else I could do. I had had it.

Something had to give.

I needed the Lord to do something.

I needed a word from the Lord.

Desperately, I went to seek His face. I stood. I waited. My ears were attentive to His voice. My eyes waited with expectancy as I looked for Him.

I just needed a word; just "one" word from the Lord.

I was extremely uncomfortable; my spirit was restless.

All day and all night there was a tug-of-war going on between my flesh and my spirit. I had no idea what was going on. All I knew was I needed to get in the presence of the Lord.

So I pressed.

Then He spoke.

"In nine months…" He said.

And immediately, the tears burst forth and there was a breakthrough in my spirit. He reminded me of what's going on in the spirit; a reminder of where I am.

I'm pregnant.

His words confirmed what He's doing in me; what He's birthing in my life, and immediately the enemy is defeated.

Instantly, the tug-of-war is over! He revealed the tug-of-war was because the enemy was trying to stop me from doing what God has called me to do; the baby is growing.

And the breakthrough launches me to a new level in God!

The tears continued to roll down my face as I allowed the Lord to have His way with me.
I couldn't help but be reminded of God giving David the victory: When the Philistines heard that David had been anointed king of Israel, they mobilized all their forces to capture him. The Lord gave the enemy into David's hand.

So David went to Baal-perazim and defeated the Philistines there. "The LORD did it!" David exclaimed. "He burst through my enemies like a raging flood!" So

he named that place Baal-perazim (which means "the Lord who bursts through").

2 Samuel 5:20 NLT

My enemies had mobilized against me, but had been defeated; given into my hands!

I am on another level!

Glory be to God – "The Lord of the Breakthrough!"

You're uncomfortable and restless because you are on the verge of a breakthrough!

The tug-of-war between your flesh and your spirit is the enemy trying to keep you from moving forward.

But God is getting ready to give you the victory!

God is getting ready to burst through in your life!

He is getting ready to take you to another level!

The baby is growing.

You've outgrown the place that you're in.

You can't stay there.

It's time to go to another level.

He is "The Lord of the Breakthrough!"

PRESS INTO GOD...AND HE'LL BURST THROUGH FOR YOU!

INCREASE!

That ye might walk worthy of the Lord unto all pleasing, being fruitful in every good work, and increasing in the knowledge of God;

Colossians 1:10 KJV

Week 20
May 13 – May 19

"DON'T FORGET!"

When I went to bed, I expected the Lord to speak. I expected Him to reveal Himself to me.

In a dream…

As I slept, the Lord said,

"Don't forget what you wanted to be." His words rung out in my spirit loud and clear.

When I woke up, immediately I thought of how often we become who, what other people want us to be, ask us to be, and even demand us to be. And in doing so, how we've lost ourselves, and have gotten tangled up in other people's expectations, ideals of who they want us to be.

And I thought about how we've lost ourselves time and time again trying to fill their shoes of expectation.

The reality of losing the dream, desire, and hunger to become who the Lord has created us to be reminded me of that person who I had become; who was once buried deep down inside. And the years I spent trying to find my way out. Years of trying to find out who I really was. Years of trying to dig myself out from under all of the hurt, pain, disappointment, and discouragement that I found myself buried in.

[82]

I was saddened by the fact that this is the case for many of us: you've lost your motivation to dream, your will to become who God has created you to become. Because you too can't seem to shake the person that you've become; the person who's buried deep down inside. And the years you've spent trying to find your way out, the years you've spent trying to find out who you really are, the years you've spent trying to dig yourself out from under all of the hurt, pain, disappointment, and discouragement that you've found yourself buried in.

And consequently, up until now, we never got the chance to be who we really wanted to be.

Often times, in our search to satisfy that intrinsic hunger of who we were created to be, who God created us to become; that dream that was knitted into the fibers of our beings, somehow we continue to see it. We continue to hope. And something inside whispers, "That's who I am."

After a little pondering, I couldn't help but be reminded of my own dream; the dream that reminds me that only God can do it (because there's no way I can do it on my own). You know, the dream that's waaay out of my reach – that impossible dream.

The dream of who I am.

And yet, I'm excited because one thing is clear. The Lord isn't saying, "Don't forget..." just to be saying it. (I hope you didn't miss what I said, "up until now.")

Because God is getting ready to bring it to pass! He's getting ready to make it happen.

He has not forgotten you!

My God! I'm sooo excited!

The Lord is saying remember what it is that you wanted to be. He's saying don't overlook what it is that you wanted to be, don't neglect what it is that you wanted to be, and, continuously work towards that.

He's going to bring it to pass!

You will become all that He has created you to be.

That dream that's inside of you, that hunger that's inside of you...He put it there!

He is reminding you: Don't forget! Don't give up! Don't lose hope!

Continue to work towards the dream.

God has not forgotten about you!

It will manifest soon.

INCREASE!

The wise in heart shall be called prudent: and the sweetness of the lips increaseth learning.

Proverbs 16:21 KJV

I'M EXPECTING!

I had come to a crossroad.

My only question: What do I do?

Immediately, I was reminded that I had been here before: I've been in this same situation once before. And just as suddenly, I was also reminded that it wasn't like before. It was different.

I was in the same situation, but things had changed, circumstances had changed.

The one difference that stood out the most was: the first time it happened, I found myself in that situation after a very difficult time. This time, however, I had willingly given everything up to be in His will.

And yet, I was still faced with the same situation.

This time, however, I wasn't afraid. I wasn't concerned.

The one thing that was the same was: I had no idea what was going to happen.

But what I did know was: I am expecting!

The spirit of expectation had overtaken me! And now I'm expecting God to show up and show out! I am expecting

Him to prove Himself once again! Because I've seen Him work!

When I came to this crossroad once before, the Lord saw me through. He made ways out of no ways and created doors where there were no doors. He did it then and He'll do it now.

I'm excited because I know it's going to be something good! It's going to be something that I could not do for myself. It's going to be something big; something huge! It's going to be a blessing that's beyond what I could ever imagine or think!

God's going to do it!

I can't help but be reminded that I have given up everything as His word rings out in my spirit,

"And everyone who has given up houses or brothers or sisters or father or mother or children or property, for my sake, will receive a hundred times as much in return and will inherit eternal life."
Matthew 19:29 NLT

You see, I'm expecting a hundredfold!

A hundredfold?

Yes! Not thirty or sixty, but a hundredfold!

I'm expecting the Lord to give me back far more than I've given up: houses, brothers, sisters, father, mother, children and property, for His sake. I'm expecting the Lord's blessings to manifest; His word to manifest!

A hundredfold!

I believe there is no way that I've come to this place (where the Lord had given me victory) and there not be a blessing waiting for me. Therefore, it's not really a crossroad, but rather an opportunity for the Lord to show Himself strong and mighty in my life. All I have to do is continue to wait on Him with expectancy! Then receive!

How many times have we come face to face with what seemed to be the impossible? So often we find ourselves in what we believe to be a difficult situation because we can't see our way out. But there is nothing too hard for God. And nothing is impossible for Him.

Too often we get overwhelmed with our situations or circumstances because we rely on our own resources, strategies, and wisdom, which often fail us. And in doing so, all we can see is the gloom and doom (instead of looking at the situation as an opportunity for God to bless us)! An opportunity for Him to prove Himself once again!

Take your eyes off of the situation, put your eyes on God, and watch Him work! Watch Him turn your situation around and work it out for your good!

You're not at a crossroad!

You're in a place to receive a hundredfold!

There is no way the Lord is going to let you out-give Him!

All that you've given up for the sake of the gospel; for the sake of being in His will!

Stop looking at your situation as if there's no way that it can be figured out! As if it's impossible! Instead, clothe yourself with a spirit of expectancy! Expect the Lord to fix it for you! Expect the Lord to turn it around for you! Expect the Lord to do the impossible! Expect Him to pour out a blessing that you don't have room to receive! Expect Him to give you back more than you've given up!

Expect a hundredfold!

And watch Him do it!

INCREASE!

And the man increased exceedingly, and had much cattle, and maidservants, and menservants, and camels, and asses.

Genesis 30:43 KJV

WHERE IS YOUR FAITH?

I don't know how I've lived in Orlando and hadn't taken advantage of the tourist attractions. (Well, maybe it's because I'm not a tourist.) Anyway, I couldn't help but take advantage of the opportunity when my son came home from Kuwait; after all, he was on vacation.

Anyway, I thought this would be the perfect thing for us to do because it offered a number of activities all in one place. One of the activities that was offered was a "rope course" (twenty different obstacles).

As soon as I heard about the rope obstacle, I was all in. And immediately, my militant mind started to image what the rope obstacle would entail. So, I imagined it would be like the obstacle courses that are offered at military boot camps.

I wouldn't mind getting dirty, crawling on my stomach under the ropes that hung ever so slightly above me. I wouldn't mind having to jump, grab the rope, and use my feet to climb over the wall. I wouldn't mind having to double-dutch through the rope hoops as I made my way to the other end. I wouldn't mind having to swing from one rope to another as if swinging from the monkey bars.

Besides, my son is the Marine that he is because I taught him everything he knows (I bragged).

So after we had done all the activities that were offered, I was more than excited to get to the rope obstacle.

I was ready!

We made it to the obstacle course. There were people everywhere (involved in yet more activities that were offered). The closer we got to the entrance, the more excited I got. Then, for some strange reason, something caught my attention above my head. And I looked up.

As I looked up, there was a young man who was looking down (seemingly directly at me) as he made his way through the apparent rope obstacle - thirty-six feet up in the air.

Wait!

What?

I stood there. This was not what I had imagined! And yet, somehow I was still excited about doing the course; only now, I had no idea how it was going to happen.

Then it was my turn. The attendant strapped me into a harness and hooked the lever that was attached to the harness into the rail that hung above my head. The only thing I had to hold on to was the rope that connected me to the lever above.

And somehow, as his words assured me that I was done with the safety check, my nerves started to set in as I walked up the stairs to the obstacle course that was about thirty-six feet above the people who were involved in the activities.

Slowly, nervously, I made it to the top. Now the uncertainty that I was feeling as I walked up the stairs to determine whether or not I should be doing this, became very clear by the time I made it to the top.

I was certain that I should not be doing this.

And instantly, the fear started to overtake me as I looked out at the course that was before me. And immediately, it was clear that there wasn't anything to hold on to but the rope that was attached to my harness, and there wasn't a net below.

I was getting ready to walk out on seemingly nothing!

I stood there.

As I tried to gather my nerves and overcome the fear that was threatening me to turn around and go back down the stairs and just take the harness off, I tried to figure out how to get across the course. The course that was before me had two rails (maybe a foot-and-a-half apart) that I had to walk across to get to the other side. Sounds easy enough, right?

Well, the only thing that kept it from being easy was the fact that again, I had nothing to hold on to and when I looked down, the thirty-six feet in the air reminded me that there wasn't a net below. It was terrifying, and all I could think about was the fear of falling. But I had to do it. I hadn't come to not go through with it. So, I made up my mind that I was going to just make it happen.

The only thing with that was, my head and my feet weren't in agreement; my head was saying go, but my feet wouldn't move. Again, I contemplated just turning around and going back downstairs. A few quick words of encouragement and somehow like a baby taking their first steps, I stood there with just one foot on the rail and the other on the landing (as I waited for my other foot to take the second step). And before I knew anything, I was calling on Jesus. "Lord, help me." With each step that I took I said, "Jesus, help me. Lord, I know you've got me." And before I knew anything I had made it to the other side. "Whew! Thank you, Jesus!"

Suspension bridges, swinging beams, lily pads – each course was the same.

The first baby step, "Lord, help me." The second step, "Jesus…Lord, I know you got me." And again, somehow I made it, "Whew! Thank you, Jesus!"

We made it through six of the twenty different courses before our allotted time was up.

And while each course was different, my approach remained the same.

That night, I couldn't help but think about the courses as the Lord began to minister to me and revealed how the courses are just like our walk with Him.

He revealed that each course is reflective of the different struggles we encounter in life.

How many times are we faced with situations that seemingly there's no way we're going to make it to the other side? How many obstacles do we face and there's still fear and trepidation? Better yet, how many times have we come face to face with an obstacle and somehow we make it through? Obstacles where we know there's nothing to hold on to and there's no net below. And yet, we face each one with the same approach:

We fail to realize that we're connected above.

It's a different challenge, but you treat it the same, "Lord, help me. Jesus, help me. Lord, I know you got it."

One step, two steps. Put one foot in front of the other. You made it.

"Whew! Thank you, Jesus!"

While it may be frightening, it also shows our lack of trust. This is what we do instead of walking by faith.

The Lord said, "Trust Me."

It doesn't matter what obstacle you may face. He'll see you through.

So every time you're faced with an obstacle, all you have to do is trust Him. Trust that you're connected above. And while it may appear to be no one or nothing to hold onto, remember, He's always there.

There is no way that you can fall – you're connected.

Walk by faith not by sight!

INCREASE!

And the children of Israel were fruitful, and increased abundantly, and multiplied, and waxed exceeding mighty; and the land was filled with them.

Exodus 1:7 KJV

FORESEE A STORM?

I tossed and turned; couldn't sleep.

Awakened; I prayed.

"Peace, be still," the Lord said.

Immediately I was overtaken by His peace.

And he arose, and rebuked the wind, and said unto the sea, Peace, be still. And the wind ceased, and there was a great calm. (Mark 4:39)

I was reminded of the revelation of this passage of scripture: the fact that the Lord said, "Let us pass over unto the other side" (in verse 35) meant no matter what happened in between point A and point B; they would make it to the other side!

He assured me that He would get me to my expected end.

Assured that I would come out of the storm victoriously; I would make it to the other side of the storm.

While I always remember that I'll make it to the other side, I sometimes forget not to worry. I forget not to become concerned; not to anticipate the worse; not to toss and turn in my sleep. Sometimes, I forget that Jesus is on board, like the disciples did.

You see, this storm was designed to work in us the "expected end."

So it doesn't matter what we're going through; it doesn't matter how hard the winds blow or the waves beat against us we'll make it to the other side because the Lord said so.

So whatever you have to face on the way, face it. Whatever you have to go through on the way, go through it. Whatever you have to let go of, let it go.

The way is already made.

The storm is designed to work out of us what needs to be worked out; you know, the fear, doubt, worry, concern, and oh, yeah, the lack of faith.

This storm is not about the house; it's not about the car; it's not about the finances; it's not about the job; it's not about the relationship.

This storm is about your faith!

Do you trust Him? Do you believe He'll do what He said He'll do? Do you believe He'll make a way for you? Do you believe you'll make it to the other side?

Do you believe He'll get you to your expected end?

The Lord asked the disciples, "Why are you so fearful? How is it that you have no faith?"

Why are you afraid?

Do you foresee a storm? Do you think you're going to be overtaken? Do you believe Jesus is on board?

The storm is to prepare you for the expected end: faith in Him!

I rebuke the winds and say to the water, "Peace. Be Still!" And the fear, worry, doubt, concern, and confusion shall cease and a great calm is released. In the name of Jesus.

There is no need to fear – Jesus is on board.

Have faith!

Let the chips fall where they may.

If He does it, it's all good.

If He doesn't, it's all good.

Trust Him! He will get you to your expected end.

INCREASE!

Hast not thou made an hedge about him, and about his house, and about all that he hath on every side? thou hast blessed the work of his hands, and his substance is increased in the land.

Job 1:10 KJV

UNTAPPED POTENTIAL

I remember when we first started out in ministry, and how difficult it had become. We were doing everything that we could imagine doing as we prepared for the ministry to start.

We had started to evangelize. We had done the community outreach; turkeys for Thanksgiving and toys for Christmas.

We preached the word of God.

But what was frustrating was we didn't have anyone helping us.

And no matter how hard we tried to keep going, it was always difficult when we thought about how no one had come to support us.

We prayed to *the Lord of the Harvest,* asking Him to send the laborers.

And still, no one came.

Finally, we had gotten to a place of peace. We knew the Lord would send the people, we just had to wait until they came; we had to be patient. We knew that it would happen in the Lord's timing – not ours.

Then suddenly and from out of nowhere it seemed as though it all just hit me like a ton of bricks. My spirit had become so heavy. Desperate. And I found myself just crying out to God.

The frustration had made its way front and center.

"I just want to know if we're in the right vein," I cried out.

It didn't matter how long it would take for the people to come. Or even if they came – I just wanted to know if we were doing what *He* wanted us to do, and not doing what we *thought* we should've been doing. As long as we were in His will, all was well.

We realized we were frustrated because we couldn't seem to figure out how we were supposed to get to that next level. But as we continue to seek the Lord, He revealed:

(1) We were in the right place.
(2) There was some untapped potential in the place that we were in.

That's why we couldn't go to the next level. That's why we couldn't leave the place we were in.

It all made sense.

✓ While we were focused on getting to the next level, God was focused on what He wanted us to do in the place that we were in. There was more He wanted us to do where we were.
✓ While we were focused on getting to the next level, in essence, *we* wanted to do something that wasn't for us to do, in that season.

[102]

✓ While we were focused on getting to the next level, there were so many opportunities for us that we hadn't tapped into, in the place that we were in.

It was then that we realized what we were supposed to be doing – in the place that we were in. It was then that we realized that there was so much more that we could do – in the place that we were in. It was then that we realized that we really hadn't even scratched the surface – in the place that we were in.

There was so much more for us to do.

Sometimes, we can get so caught up with what we want; sometimes we can get so caught up with what everybody else is doing that we miss what God is trying to do in and through us.

So, let me just say this: "You're in that place for a reason." And my suggestion to you is this: Don't be in such a hurry to leave that place because God has you there for a reason. He's using that place to develop you. He's using that place to accomplish His will.

More than likely, you haven't even began to scratch the surface of what He wants you to do. There's so much more you can do in that place.

So I pray that God will open your eyes, ears, and heart so that you may see, hear and receive what it is that He's doing in your life, in this season. I pray that you will be content in that place and do all that He has called you to do.

You are right where He wants you to be.

There is so much untapped potential in that place.

INCREASE!

Thou hast put gladness in my heart, more than in the time that their corn and their wine increased.

Psalm 4:7 KJV

YOUR HAIR IS GROWING

In a dream…

As I looked in the mirror, I could see my hair growing. It was just past my waist. I was excited and amazed at how long it had grown.

Now we all know that hair is a very sensitive subject for a lot of people; women in particular. And we've gone to great lengths in search of our identity as we've struggled with who we are; as a result of our hair.

Anyway, when I thought of "hair growing," I couldn't help but be reminded of Samson in Judges, chapter sixteen, verse twenty-two:

But the hair on his head began to grow again after it had been shaved.

In this verse, which may be a very familiar passage of scripture to most of us, we know that Samson's long hair was a sign that he was a Nazirite, wholly given to God (which meant no razor had ever been used on his head because he had been set apart to God since birth). And it was a sign of his trust and belief in God, and His commandments.

[105]

Now we may not have taken an oath to become a Nazirite as Samson had, but we did, nonetheless, take an oath to trust and obey the Lord's commandments (when we were saved by His grace).

And since then, some of us may have done some things that we shouldn't have done, like Samson, by telling Delilah the secret of his strength. And ultimately we, like Samson, have since been overpowered and subdued by the enemy.

You know that *one time too many* you said something that you shouldn't have said; that *one time too many* you did something that you shouldn't have done; that *one time too many* you went somewhere you know you shouldn't have gone; only to find yourself wrapped up and tied up, defeated.

And the Lord had departed from him.

And the Lord had given you over to the enemy.

While He knew that if his hair had been cut, he would become as weak as any other man; he had yet to come to the understanding that *the Lord was his strength.* You see, often times we think that we can continue to do what we're doing and the Lord will be there. Not so! While we understand that the Lord will never leave nor forsake us, we have yet to come to the understanding that the Lord's presence in our lives is reflective of our obedience to Him.

Now, with that being said, the good news is, the bible tells us that *before long...*Samson's hair began to grow back!

So, I've come to share with you:

The interpretation of the dream…

After all that you've been through, like Samson, your hair is growing! The presence of the Lord is returning to you! Your strength is returning to you!

Amen!?

Now you're able to overtake and subdue the enemy.

Like Samson, God's going to give you the strength, the power to destroy your enemy.

Your greatest victory yet, is about to happen!

INCREASE!

Be not thou afraid when one is made rich, when the glory of his house is increased;

Psalm 49:16 KJV

STAND

The time that we'd been waiting for had finally come. We were excited in our spirits and had declared and decreed that no devil in hell would be able to stop us from doing what God had called us to do. We were walking by faith, and would continue to do so no matter what happened.

We believed God. And that settled it.

As we started to move forward, seemingly my friend seemed to waver. And immediately I was concerned that they may not be on board with what we had been declaring. But I continued. And the further we went, the more I became concerned that they may not be walking by faith. Somehow all I heard was doubt (but I was determined to move forward come hell or high water). But my spirit was disturbed, so I said, "I'm concerned that you may not be on board. Your actions are indicating that you may not be all in."

I was assured that they were all in.

I continued to move forward in what "we" believed the Lord had prompted us to do. A door that we had been praying that God would open, had been opened. And now I was moving forward in cultivating the blessing so that the harvest would come; so that the harvest would be plentiful.

Again, I was met with resistance as I was questioned about my ability to make this happen. Then, an all-out attack (though subtle), hidden in words disguised as "I'm just asking," started to question *my* ability to make this happen. Even questioned if I had somehow gotten off track; lost focus of what it was that I was supposed to be doing.

And with little hesitation, I answered the accusations as I defended my position of trying to take advantage of every opportunity that the Lord had given me. But I have to admit, my defense was met with great concern of what was happening.

I entered into the Lord's presence and began to pray. I quickly gave the situation to the Lord as I had become concerned and confused as I asked Him what was going on; and asked what I should do to move forward.

Then I waited for His response.

The word of the Lord came to me in the night.

After you have done everything, to stand.

When I woke up, the peace of the Lord was upon me as He began to give me understanding concerning His word and the situation. Immediately, He wanted me to understand that the important thing for me to do was *to stand*.

He revealed to me "to stand" means to remain unchanged; steadfast and unmovable.
As the word was revealed, I was strengthened and encouraged in my spirit, and knew without a shadow of a doubt I was on the right path and doing what the Lord had told me to do.

Then the Lord continued to minister to me as I remained in His presence.

And immediately I could see the enemy using this individual in an attempt to keep me from doing what the Lord had called me to do; to keep me from getting what the Lord said I could have. And just as suddenly, I was reminded of the enemy's tactic: attacking *my* ability to get it done.

Therefore, my brothers and my sisters, I want to declare to you today the word of the Lord:

After you have done everything, to stand.

Remain unchanged; steadfast and unmovable.

Stand on His word!

Continue to walk by faith!

Continue to stand in agreement with the word of God: You are what it says you are. You can do what it says you can do. You can have what it says you can have. You can go where it says you can go.

Let us be mindful that while the Lord has given the blessing to us, often times we'll be met with resistance as the enemy tries to keep us from getting what God says we can have.

Stand.

Let us also be mindful that obstacles are placed in our path to see if we really want what we say we want. When met with resistance, are we going to give up? Or are we going to stand?

It doesn't matter what battle you may be facing.

We fight not against flesh and blood; the fight is not against the individual that the enemy uses, but against evil rulers and authorities of the unseen world, against mighty powers in this dark world, and against evil spirits in the heavenly places. Therefore, put on every piece of God's armor so you will be able to resist the enemy in the time of evil. Then after the battle you will still be standing firm.

Ephesians 6:12-13 NLT

Stand.

Remain unchanged.

Steadfast.

Unmovable.

It is never our ability to make the blessing happen; it is our obedience to His instructions that makes the blessing happen.

STAND.

INCREASE!

And he increased his people greatly; and made them stronger than their enemies.

Psalm 105:24 KJV

STUDY FOR THE TEST

As I listened to the man of God minister, the Spirit of the Lord came upon me and began to minister to me.

Immediately and loud and clear, the Lord said, "Study for the test."

And instantly I was reminded of my English class during my freshman year in high school. Every week, we'd have a list of vocabulary words that we had to study then we'd be tested on Friday. Week in and week out it was the same.

Now I have to say that I loved the vocabulary words; I loved going over them in class. But I also have to say that while I loved the vocabulary words because they seemed to empower me, I did not; I repeat I did not like taking the test.

Why?

I hadn't studied.

As I looked back, I shook my head in disappointment as I was reminded that week in and week out I had barely passed the tests. And now what's more disturbing is the fact that it was okay to barely get by. It was okay to score just enough to pass.

You see, I barely passed the tests because I never studied the words. I went off of my memory. I used the "word association" method to past the tests. That is, when a particular word was used in the definition, I knew which word it was associated with. But I never studied the words to understand the meaning of the word.

But today, my sisters and my brothers, the Lord is saying, "Study to show thyself approved unto God."

Study to show thyself approved unto God, a workman that needeth not to be ashamed, rightly dividing the word of truth.

2 Timothy 2:15 KJV

To study means to carefully examine a subject.

So I'm here to tell you that it doesn't matter what you're going through; it doesn't matter what test you're faced with, you have to study for the test!

Study the word of God; examine carefully what the word of God is saying concerning your test. Examine: test by questioning the word of God concerning that which you are going through.

Your first question: "Lord, what are you saying concerning my situation?"

It doesn't matter what situation you may be faced with; the answer is in the Word.

If you're going through financially; examine the subject carefully. What does the word say about financial freedom? Prosperity? Wealth? If you're being tested physically, in your body, examine the subject carefully. What does the word say about healing?

While going through this test, you can do what I used to do and use "word association" and not have any understanding of the word. You may think what you know about the word is enough. But I'm here to tell you that if that's the case, you'll only prolong the test.

It's not until you get an understanding of the word, study the word, examine the subject carefully that pleases God.

When you declare and decree the word of God, you are holding God accountable to perform His word.

You get an understanding, you get the answers, and you pass the test!

Study the word of God and do what it says.

It's up to you how soon you come out and if you pass the test or not.

Study for the test.

It is pleasing unto the Lord.

Show thyself approved unto God that you would find favor in His eyes.

Be diligent, faithful, and trustworthy.

INCREASE!

For by me thy days shall be multiplied, and the years of thy life shall be increased.

Proverbs 9:11 KJV

LET HIM PREPARE YOU

As I sat and thought about all that the Lord had given into my hands, I couldn't help but be reminded of how blessed I am that He trusts me.

And still, there are so many times when I lose sight of all that He has given me, and I wonder *when is He going to bless me?*

Now, when I say, "When is he going to bless me?" I mean *bless me with what I want* not with what He has given me. So many times I find myself wanting to do what I want to do rather than what He wants me to do.

Not that I don't want to do what He has given me to do, *but* I want to do what *I* want to do.

Sometimes I lose sight of the *purpose* of what He gave me to do. Sometimes I lose sight of the *importance* of what He gave me to do. And sometimes I lose sight of the *blessing* of what He gave me to do.

But that's all a part of the process.

The bottom line is: Sometimes, I don't want to go through the process. But I want the blessing. Sometimes, I don't want to understand the process. But I want the blessing. Sometimes, I don't want to learn or grow from the process. But I want the blessing.

[118]

But I know it doesn't matter how much I want the blessing. It doesn't matter what I do to try to get the blessing. It doesn't matter how much I pray for the blessing. I won't get the blessing until I've gone through the process.

How often do we forget that God is not really interested in the end product as much as He's interested in us going through the process?

It is during the process that we learn; grow. It is during the process that we get to know the procedure. It is during the process that we are prepared for the blessing. It is during the process that we get to know God.

Otherwise, we don't get the blessing.

Let me say this:

- ✓ We don't get the blessing *just because* we want it.
- ✓ We don't get the blessing *just because* God said we can have it.
- ✓ We don't get the blessing *just because* we've fasted and prayed for it.

We get the blessing when we've been prepared for it.

So as long as we understand that the blessing **is** ours, as long as we understand that God **wants** us to be blessed, we must also understand that we **have to** go through the process!

Just like Joseph had to go through the process, so do we:

And they said one to another, Behold, this dreamer cometh.

Come now therefore, and let us slay him, and cast him into some pit, and we will say, Some evil beast hath devoured him: and we shall see what will become of his dreams.

Genesis 37:19 – 20 KJV

The process is to provide us with revelation and faith for the difficult times. And in the end…we get to know God.

You have to go through in order to get to – the blessings.

Let Him prepare you.

Go through the process.

And receive your blessings.

INCREASE!

So I was great, and increased more than all that were before me in Jerusalem: also my wisdom remained with me.

Ecclesiastes 2:9 KJV

A SEED IN THE GROUND

Awaken.

I'm troubled in my spirit as my dream revealed I'm close to home, but I'm struggling to get there. The slightest sense of fear makes itself known as the enemy whispers, "It's not going to happen." Immediately I'm reminded of the challenge that's before me. It is my darkest hour. And I'm faced with all sorts of uncertainties.

I rush to get in the Lord's presence.

As I bow before Him, suddenly peace comes over me and soothes my spirit. He reminds me I have a seed in the ground. His words ring out in my spirit and play over and over in my mind: I have a seed in the ground. I have a seed in the ground. I have a seed in the ground.

As He speaks, He arrests my uncertainties; causing them to cease!

I started to declare the word of the Lord: "I have a seed in the ground."

Then I was reminded of how I had sown this seed in faith. I had prayed for this seed. And I had declared and decreed this seed to increase. The words released from my mouth caused a breakthrough in my spirit.

And instantly, the vision was before me:

A plant: a single stem, broken through the ground and had sprouted up.

The interpretation of the vision…

The seed I had planted in faith, had taken root, grown, broken through the ground, and had come forth.

The seed had increased. The blessing had come forth.

There had been a breakthrough in the spirit.

I could clearly see that there was a "break" in the ground, which is reflective of the breakthrough (not only in the spirit), but also in the natural.

The God of the breakthrough had come to deliver increase!

THIS IS THE YEAR OF INCREASE! In every area of our lives.

ARE YOU EXPECTING INCREASE?

Are you expecting a harvest but haven't sown a seed? Sow a seed! God will give you increase!

Have you sown a seed and waiting for the increase? God will give you increase!

Let us be mindful that as we sow seeds we are careful to sow in faith. The increase comes not because we planted the seed, but because we nurture the seed: we "plant" (sow) in faith and "water" by faith (with our prayers and declarations).

IT IS THE LORD WHO GIVES THE INCREASE!

It's not important who does the planting, or who does the watering. What's important is that God makes the seed grow.

1 Corinthians 3:7 NLT

INCREASE!

INCREASE!

Look unto Abraham your father, and unto Sarah that bare you: for I called him alone, and blessed him, and increased him.

Isaiah 51:2 KJV

FIRST FRUITS

I decided I would trust God.

I could have what God says I could have.

I would have The Ties That Bind Women's Conference.

This conference was birth out of me writing my first book: The Ties That Bind.

As a result of me writing the book, I've traveled from city to city and state to state ministering as God severed the ties that have had us bound: Ungodly soul ties: sexual ties, emotional ties, spiritual ties, physical ties, psychological ties, relational ties and financial ties.

For this reason – the Lord was made manifest that He would destroy the works of the enemy. That He would heal, deliver and set us free.

The first Ties That Bind Women's Conference was held February 19, 2005. So I did not take it lightly that I was having my first conference, in Orlando, Florida, ten years later.

You see, on January 16, 2015, the Lord dropped in my spirit to have this conference. And immediately I was excited in my spirit. And just as suddenly as I had received the revelation, the enemy told me that there was no way that I could have a conference.

So I sowed a seed that following Sunday and named it "The Ties That Bind Women's Conference - 2015."

And immediately I put the plan into action. I started looking for a place and allowed God to dictate who, what, when, where, and how I should have the conference.

Less than a month after sowing the seed, the Lord revealed to me that the seed I had planted had broken through the ground and had come forth! The promise; the blessing had manifested itself in the spirit.

And on February 20, 2015, the promise; the blessing manifested itself in the natural!

And I had the very conference that the enemy said I couldn't have.

But I didn't celebrate because the enemy said I couldn't have the conference.

I celebrated because of the prophetic word of the Lord that was shared with me, "This conference belonged to Him."

As the Lord continued to minister to me, He made it clear that this conference, the first, Ties That Bind Women's Conference, belonged to Him.

It was my first fruit unto Him.

As excited as I was to have the conference, as excited as I was to share how the Lord had come in and showed out at the conference, as excited as I was to share the messages that were preached during the conference, the Lord said, "It all belongs to Me."

I recorded the conference, recorded the messages that were preached. I recorded everything to share the anointing and the presence of God that was in that place, but the Lord said, "It belongs to Me."

So, when the Lord showed up and showed out, it was ONLY for the people who were there. When the word of the Lord was ministered, it was ONLY for the people who were there. Everything that had been recorded was ONLY for the people who were there.

This conference was between God and the people He ordained to be in that place at that appointed time. This conference was NOT for the masses.

It was only for the people who the Lord ordained to be a part of the conference.

The blessings, the breakthrough that was in the place was for the people who God had chosen to be there to receive. God had a divine appointment with His people.

The first fruit belongs to God.

And the feast of harvest, the firstfruits of thy labours, which thou hast sown in the field:

Exodus 23:16a KJV

I understood that the seed that had broken through the ground was not just about me having a conference per se, but rather it was about me having power and authority over the enemy in new realms, level and dimensions. It was about me having power and authority over new regions, new territories (here in Orlando, Florida). It was about me possessing the land that God said I could have, and had given me to possess.

I will say this, "I will never be the same after what I experienced at that conference!"

So I want to encourage you today: the first fruit belongs to God.

If you want to see increase in your life, if you want to experience the breakthrough that you need, if you want to reap a harvest, sow your seed and offer the first fruit up to God.

Give the first of your labor, the first of your harvest to the Lord.

For if the firstfruit be holy, the lump is also holy: and if the root be holy, so are the branches.

Romans 11:16 KJV

INCREASE!

Take ye wives, and beget sons and daughters; and take wives for your sons, and give your daughters to husbands, that they may bear sons and daughters; that ye may be increased there, and not diminished.

Jeremiah 29:6 KJV

Week 31
July 29 – August 4

SHIFT!

While this is the year of increase, there has been a shift in the spirit.

THIS IS A NEW SEASON!

When he had finished speaking, he said to Simon, "Put out into deep water, and let down the nets for a catch."

Simon answered, "Master, we've worked hard all night and haven't caught anything. But because you say so, I will let down the nets."

When they had so, they caught such a large number of fish that their nets began to break. So they signaled their partners in the other boat to come and help them, and they came and filled both boats so full that they began to sink.

When Simon Peter saw this, he fell at Jesus' knees and said, "Go away from me, Lord; I am a sinful man!" For he and all his companions were astonished at the catch of fish they had taken, and so were James and John, the sons of Zebedee, Simon's partners.

Then Jesus said to Simon, "Don't be afraid; for now on you will catch men."

Luke 5:4 – 11 NIV

I'm sure the above-mentioned scripture reference is a very familiar passage of scriptures because we all want increase; we all want abundance.

However, I'm afraid that we're so focused on the deep; we're so focused on the net; we're so focused on the catch, that we have yet to get a revelation of who Jesus really is!

There was only one person who got the revelation of who Jesus was, and that was Peter! The scripture tells us that when Peter saw this, when He saw the miracle, the supernatural provision, he fell at Jesus' knees. In other words, he didn't just see an abundance, Peter had a revelation of who Jesus really was!

In this season, we must come to the understanding that the miracles, the supernatural provisions are so that we can get a revelation of who Jesus is.

In this season, God wants to reveal Himself to you! So if all you see is provision, you will never see The Provider.

Jesus spoke to the one who got the revelation: It's time to shift from catching fish to catching men! Shift! Get a revelation of who Jesus is!

INCREASE!

And there was an enlarging, and a winding about still upward to the side chambers: for the winding about of the house went still upward round about the house: therefore the breadth of the house was still upward, and so increased from the lowest chamber to the highest by the midst.

Ezekiel 41:7 KJV

THE LORD SAID, "I HAVE HEALED YOU."

I found myself in unfamiliar territory, but I was hungry for God.

I was willing to go where I had never gone. I was willing to do what I had never done, in order to see God and receive from Him in a way that I had never seen or received from Him before.

I wanted more of God.

I was tired of the status quo. I was tired of doing the same ol' things; tired of saying the same ol' things. I was ready for something new in my life! And I was expecting God to usher me into a new atmosphere of His glory.

I knew God was doing something, but I didn't know what. I thought I had an idea, but I had no clue what was getting ready to happen. I was thinking one thing and God was thinking another. I was thinking "me," God was thinking "the people."

I went in with one expectation and came out with something all together different.

But I was expecting!

I found it very difficult to comprehend what He was doing. I struggled. The atmosphere was confusing. I had to keep encouraging myself and reminding myself that I was there for a reason. And hopefully sooner rather than later God would reveal His purpose and plan.

I pressed.

Suddenly, and from out of nowhere, He made His plan known. I was arrested in my spirit. I didn't come here for that, I thought to myself. Then I realized He wanted to manifest His supernatural power. Well, you better answer, I reasoned with myself.

So, I answered.

And it wasn't until then that I got the revelation that God wanted to do something for me that I hadn't asked Him to do. But I struggled because I was in unfamiliar territory. And while I had acknowledged His presence and His power, I prepared myself to receive.

The power of God came upon me and before I knew anything I was laying prostrate before Him; He wanted to demonstrate His power in my life.

The Lord spoke, "I have healed you."

And as the prophetic word was released, it released the revelation of the Lord, the timing of the Lord, and the power and virtue of the Lord.

In other words: IT'S ALREADY DONE.

The Lord said, "I have healed you." And in the timing of the Lord, His power and virtue will be displayed in your life. And it WILL manifest!

How is it that we don't know what God is doing in our lives? How is it that we don't know what God is doing in the earth? The things that He's doing in our lives and the things that He's doing in the earth are revealed to us by divine revelation. It's because we have to receive from Him by divine revelation. They have to be revealed to us, and we have to come into agreement with what He's doing in order for His manifested power and glory to be revealed.

Allow me to say this: Sometimes, God will allow things to manifest supernaturally, but then there are times when He allows them to manifest naturally. There are also times when He allows them to manifest immediately, but then there are times when they manifest in time.

For example:

If you've ever experienced sickness or disease in your body and you've just dealt with it, not really thinking anything of it. I mean, it's not life threatening or anything like that, but it has become something that you've just learned to live with. When you're in an environment where God wants to heal you, and you feel lead to come under the anointing that's being released, God is ushering you into His presence so that He can bring healing to your body. If by chance you find yourself under the power of the Holy Spirit, and yet the sickness or disease is still there, that doesn't mean that you haven't been healed.

Sometimes it's not about you getting healed right then and there (supernaturally). Sometimes, it's about God letting you know that He's aware of your situation, and that He wants you to come into agreement with what He's doing, so that He can heal you (in time). Ultimately, it's about you being able to manifest His supernatural healing power in the earth to bring healing to the body of Christ.

What am I saying?

Sometimes, when God makes known that He wants to heal you, He wants you to come into agreement with Him in that particular area of healing. Then, it is His desire that you would search Him for the healing – search His word, meditate on His word, understand His healing power, activate your faith, and allow Him to manifest the healing in your life. And ultimately, this same power that was used to heal you, you'll use to heal others in the body of Christ. *And by His stripes you are healed.*

Isaiah 53:5 NKJV

Allow me to say this: However He chooses to heal you, make no mistake - YOU ARE HEALED!

God is doing a new thing in you. And He's doing a new thing in the earth. He wants to manifest His glory in the earth and wants to use you to do it. And consequently, He wants to reveal Himself to you. He wants you to get a revelation of who He is; the Healer. He wants you to get a revelation of His supernatural power and glory.

So what do you do now?

Get in His presence. Get in His word. Find all the scriptures you can that pertains to healing, meditate on them day and night, and stand on His word (no matter how long it takes); until God's healing is manifested in your life.

He sent His word and healed them,

Psalm 107:20a NKJV

INCREASE!

But thou, O Daniel, shut up the words, and seal the book, even to the time of the end: many shall run to and fro, and knowledge shall be increased.

Daniel 12:4 KJV

A "SNEAK PEEK"

While I was in the presence of the Lord, He started to minister to me. And immediately the vision was before me.

In a vision...

What appeared to be a bright light shining down from heaven quickly became the outline of an ultrasound. I could see the baby in the ultrasound. Then suddenly, there were several flashes of the baby in different positions (as if pictures of the baby were being taken, just like with an ultrasound).

The only thing that I could say was, "Wooow. Wooow," as I looked on with amazement.

I was astonished as I patiently waited for the Lord to reveal what He was saying. Then He revealed to me that what I was seeing was the "uterus." Now we understand that the uterus is also known as the "womb" of the female reproductive system, which is responsible for the development of the baby during pregnancy.

As His word was before me, I couldn't help but be reminded of what an ultrasound is. And how for the most part, it gives us a "sneak peek" of the baby growing inside the womb. And for the enjoyment of the parents, the ultrasound develops images of the baby; images of what's going on inside the body.

[140]

And immediately I got excited!

In a flash, I saw what God was doing in my life. In several pictures, I saw the plans of God for my life. In several images, I saw what the Lord is developing in my womb, spiritually.

I had a "sneak peek" of the baby that's growing inside my womb!

As I continued to sit before Him, a "sneak peek" continuously rang out in my spirit.

God is getting ready to give you a "sneak peek" of what He's doing in your life! He's getting ready to show you what He's developing in your life. He's getting ready to show you what He has in store for you; the blessings He has in store for you!

For I know the plans I have for you," says the Lord. "They are plans for good and not for disaster, to give you a future and a hope.

Jeremiah 29:11 NLT

Now we must not forget: the ultrasound gives us a glimpse of what we cannot see with the natural eye. Therefore, God allows us to "see it" via an ultrasound, in the spirit.

I pray that God opens your eyes that you may see what He's developing in your life; that you may see what He's birthing in your life.

Yes, we see the end in the beginning, so that He gives us a future, and a hope; an expected end. He gives us "sneak peeks," "glimpses" of the promises until we receive the promises.

Get ready for your "sneak peek!"

INCREASE!

And other fell on good ground, and did yield fruit that sprang up and increased; and brought forth, some thirty, and some sixty, and some an hundred.

Mark 4:8 KJV

THE POWER TO GET WEALTH

There is nothing more powerful than the word of God, the blessings of God manifesting in our lives.

However, sometimes we're so focused on what we want, what the blessing should look like, and how we think it should happen that we miss what God is doing in our lives.

And for this reason, we can't see the blessings of the Lord manifested in our lives.

We're looking for the wealth.

But thou shalt remember the LORD thy God: for it is he that giveth thee power to get wealth, that he may establish his covenant which he sware unto thy fathers, as it is this day.

Deuteronomy 8:18 KJV

He has given us the ability to get the wealth. So while we're looking for wealth to fall into our laps, the gifts and talents that He has given us; the ability that He has given us goes unused.

I know sometimes it's difficult. I know sometimes it's hard.

I know we struggle to stay focused. We struggle to remain obedient. We struggle to stay faithful. And I also know that we don't see blessings manifesting because we don't understand the plans and purposes of God for our lives. But I want to tell you that as long as you stay focused, as long as you remain obedient, and as long as you stay faithful, God will reveal His plans and purposes to you.

So shall my word be that goeth forth out of my mouth: it shall not return unto me void, but it shall accomplish that which I please, and it shall prosper in the thing whereto I sent it.

Isaiah 55:11 KJV

His word will not return to Him void.

The word may appear to be void, empty, powerless, and/or unfulfilled because it's not accomplishing what we want it to accomplish. But the word isn't void, it isn't empty, it isn't powerless, and/or unfulfilled. You see, the problem is that we want the word to accomplish what we want it to accomplish. But that's not going to happen.

His word will accomplish what He established it to accomplish.

His word is filled with His promises. It is accomplished in His timing. And it accomplishes what He wants it to accomplish.

How is it that we're not seeing the word of God accomplished or manifested in our lives?

Well, the word is being accomplished, we just don't see it. We don't see the purpose.

For as the rain cometh down, and the snow from heaven, and returneth not thither, but watereth the earth, and maketh it bring forth and bud, that it may give seed to the sower, and bread to the eater:

Isaiah 55:10 KJV

When God sends the rain and the snow, it accomplishes its purpose by watering the ground, which allows the seeds that have been planted to come forth.

Do we just see the rain and snow with no purpose?

Have you planted any seeds in order for them to grow from the rain that the Lord has sent?

I want to share a testimony with you:
A young man shared with me how he had been writing everyday and how so many times he had gotten discouraged and wanted to stop (because he didn't see any point to what he was doing). But he felt lead to keep doing it, so he pressed. And after about a year, the Lord revealed to Him that what he had been writing was the book the Lord was birthing in him.

I just want to encourage you today: Don't give up! No matter how hard it gets, don't stop doing what you're doing. In due season you will reap a harvest. Stay focused on what God has called you to do. Don't look to the left or to the right; put your blinders on and look straight ahead. Keep your eyes stayed on Jesus. He's doing a work in you and through you.

You may not understand it, but God has a purpose and a plan for your life.

He's allowing you to exercise your power; your ability to get wealth.

He's enabling you to get the wealth.

INCREASE!

And Jesus increased in wisdom and stature, and in favour with God and man.

Luke 2:52 KJV

PROMOTION...IN THE DEEP

There had been a shift in the spirit, and consequently I found myself feeling unstable, spiritually. Therefore, I knew that it wasn't by happenstance or by chance that I was lead to read the book of Luke, chapter five.

So, I read the passage of scriptures to see what the Lord was saying.

In this passage of scriptures the Lord told Peter to launch out into the deep and cast his nets. After doing so, the catch was so great that it began to break the nets. Then Peter called over his partners in the other boat to come and assist him with the catch. The catch was so abundant that they filled both boats so full that they both began to sink.

The bible tells us that when Peter saw this, he fell at the knees of Jesus and said, "Go away from me, Lord; I am a sinful man!"

Then Jesus said, "Don't be afraid! From now on you'll be fishing for people!" In other words, he would no longer catch fish, but rather he would catch men.

Then I was lead to read chapter six of the book of Luke. In this chapter, one day Jesus went into the mountain to pray, and He prayed all night. And in the morning, at daybreak, He called all of His disciples to Him. At that point, He chose twelve of them and appointed them to become apostles.

Immediately, there was something that dropped into my spirit, and caught my attention. I couldn't help but notice the similarities in both passages of scripture:

- ✓ How the Lord told them that they would no longer catch fish, but rather they would catch men.
- ✓ How the Lord told them that they would no longer be disciples, but rather they would be apostles.

Instantly, I could see them transitioning from one position to another. I could see:

- ✓ They had gone from following to now leading
- ✓ They had gone from being students to now being teachers
- ✓ They had gone from being served to now serving
- ✓ They had gone from being called to now being chosen

As I was trying to understand what was actually happening, it was clear that a shift had taken place. I could see the Lord working. I could see the Lord was doing something. And immediately, as I was reflecting on these passages of scriptures, the Lord said, "Promotion."

Wow! And suddenly it all made sense; I was being promoted. And I began to realize that I felt unstable in the spirit because I was transitioning from one position to another!

I was being promoted!

Then, I could hear the Lord say, "Launch out into the deep!"

In this season, we're not only transitioning into new positions, we are being promoted.

This shift, that is taking place now, is not a lateral move – it's a promotion!

- ✓ We're getting ready to see some things that we've never seen before.
- ✓ We're getting ready to do some things that we've never done before.
- ✓ We're getting ready to go places that we've never been before.

We're getting ready to see the manifested power of the Holy Spirit – like we've never seen before.

- ✓ You're getting ready to see Jesus in a way that you've never seen Him before.
- ✓ You're getting ready to experience Jesus in a way that you've never experienced Him before.
- ✓ You're getting ready to get to know Jesus in a way that you've never known Him before.

Launch out into the deep!

Now, I have to tell you:

- ✓ What you're looking for is in the deep.
- ✓ What you want is in the deep.
- ✓ Where you're trying to go is in the deep.
- ✓ What you want to do is in the deep

I have to also tell you:

[151]

✓ Some things can only be seen in the deep.
✓ Some things can only be received in the deep.
✓ Some things can only be revealed in the deep –
when you cast your nets.

Promotion! Promotion! Promotion!

Let us not make any mistakes. This isn't going to happen as Peter mentioned, by you toiling all night! But rather, or should I say, nevertheless, you'll have to launch out into the deep!

In order for us to go higher, we have to go deeper!

I can hear the Lord saying, "Launch out into the deep."

✓ It's time for us to transition from following to now leading.
✓ It's time for us to transition from being students to now being teachers.
✓ It's time for us to transition from being served to now serving.
✓ It's time for us to transition from being called to now being chosen.

I hear your concern: How do I launch out into the deep?

Simple: Follow Him!

INCREASE!

And the word of God increased; and the number of the disciples multiplied in Jerusalem greatly; and a great company of the priests were obedient to the faith.

Acts 6:7 KJV

Week 36
September 2 – September 8

IT'S FOR YOUR GOOD

There is nothing better than when everything seems to be going well.

Then out of nowhere, the enemy distracts you with the sole purpose of frustrating you to get your focus off of God. But I'd been in such perfect peace; the Lord's peace that when the distraction came, I quickly dismissed it. Now, let me say this, I acknowledged that the distraction was there, but I didn't get all worked up like I used to when this particular distraction found its way to my front door.

Determined to stay in God's peace, like I said, I dismissed it. But I wanted it to go away. Surely, there was an opportunity to announce the distraction in a rude and derogatory way. After all, everybody else was making known what was going wrong in their lives; the things that they were fed up with, and what they were going to do about it (if anything at all). Of course, I could jump on the band wagon and put the enemy on blast!

But I decided that I wasn't going to do that because it would've been at my own expense. Ultimately, I would've been the one who got the short end of the stick. That's why I determined that it wasn't worth it; it wasn't worth joining the band wagon. And all of a sudden, when I made the decision that I wasn't going to get on the band wagon, the Lord dropped in my spirit, "Use the 'band wagon' to minister the word of God (instead of being critical!)"

[154]

And instantly, I could see a door had been opened to allow an opportunity for the word of God to be ministered, and I walked right in.

But as for you, ye thought evil against me; but God meant it unto good, to bring to pass, as it is this day, to save much people alive.

Genesis 50:20 KJV

I know it goes without saying, but if we would just take a moment and think before we act, it'll give God the opportunity to act on our behalf. If we would just take a moment to really look at the situation before we act, it'll give us an opportunity to see God turn it around for our good. If we would just take a moment to decide to do what's right, God would open a door for us to walk right in.

There is a reason the enemy is trying to distract you. There is a reason the enemy is trying to frustrate you. There is a reason that the enemy is trying to get your focus off of God.

- ✓ He knows God is getting ready to make a way for you.
- ✓ He knows God is getting ready to give you an opportunity.
- ✓ He knows God is getting ready to open a door for you.

Therefore, if he can distract you, if he can frustrate you, if he can get you all worked up, then you won't see what God is doing, you won't see the opportunity that the Lord has for you, nor would you see the door that the Lord is opening for you.

And consequently, you'll miss the blessing God has in store for you.

Take your eyes off of your situation and put them on God.

God is turning things around for your good, do you see it?

INCREASE!

And so were the churches established in the faith, and increased in number daily.

Acts 16:5 KJV

GIVE HIM YOUR SACRIFICE

As I sit in His presence, blessed beyond measure, I'm challenged with giving back to Him for what He has given me. It was time to worship the Lord with my giving; it was offering time. There was no need to search my purse to see *how much* I would give. There was no need to search my heart to see *why* I would give. There was no need to search my conscience to see *if* I would give.

It was already clear when I left my house and headed to the house of the Lord. I knew exactly *what* I had, *how much* I had, and my conscience was clear.

I sat there in the Lord's presence and confessed to the realization that I only had three dollars. Not because that's how much I *chose* to give, not because that's what I *wanted* to give, and certainly not because I *didn't want* to give, but because *it was all that I had* to give.

I had never been in that position before.

In my disappointment, my heart was heavy because I wanted to give more. I couldn't help but be reminded of the times when I *was* in position financially and would sow seeds of thousands of dollars at a given time. But now, I was faced with not only giving three dollars, but giving all that I had.

In my displeasure, I whispered in great distress, "All I have is three dollars."

And immediately, the Lord said, "Sow that."

So, I took all that I had and gave it to the Lord; I sowed it into the Kingdom of God.

I couldn't help but be reminded of the widow woman and her two mites:

> **Then a poor widow came and dropped in two small coins.**
> **Mark 12:42 NLT**

As I meditated on this passage of scriptures the Lord began to minister to me. His words were very clear as He said to His disciples, "I tell you the truth…" and immediately, He revealed a kingdom principle.

Now, if you'll allow me to explain, anytime Jesus says, "I tell you the truth…" He's revealing a Kingdom principle. He's revealing how the Kingdom of God operates. And He went on to say that the poor widow had put *more* into the treasury than all the others. Now, here is the Kingdom principle:

It's not about the amount that you give. It's about the sacrifice that you make in order to give.

This woman gave out of her "poverty." If we look at the Webster's New World Dictionary, it tells us that poverty means *the condition or quality of being poor; need.* In other words, this woman gave out of her need; she made a sacrifice, and denied herself – putting all of her trust in Jesus to meet her needs.

Now, I'd like to back up for a minute because I don't want to miss the absolute most important part. The scripture tells us that Jesus sat down opposite the place where the offerings were put and *watched*. Let me say that again, *watched* the people putting their money into the temple treasury.

So, I'm saying that to say, He's watching what you put in the "bucket" when it passes. He sees what you're putting in the "offering plate" when it passes. And most importantly, He *knows* the condition of your heart when you give.

He knows if you're making a sacrifice or not. He knows if you're giving out of your wealth – out of your plenty or if you're giving out of your poverty – your need.

Now I would be amiss if I didn't share with you what He also revealed to me: The scripture tells us that after the widow woman had given her two mites, He called the disciples over to Him and shared with them what He saw. Basically, telling them to take notice of what she had done.

Immediately, the vision was before me:

I could see Him sitting at the right hand of the Father, watching what we put in the offering, and telling the Father to take notice.

Let us be mindful that He sees all and He knows all.

It is not the amount that you give – it's the sacrifice you make so that you can give.

Give Him everything that you have!

Make a sacrifice, and give it to Him!

[160]

Give out of your poverty; give out of your need.

And you would give Him more than anyone who gives out of their wealth.

INCREASE!

Not boasting of things without our measure, that is, of other men's labours; but having hope, when your faith is increased, that we shall be enlarged by you according to our rule abundantly,

2 Corinthians 10:15 KJV

Week 38
September 16 – September 22

UNDER AN OPEN HEAVEN

I was arrested in my spirit as I meditated in this passage of scripture and the revelation that I received:

One of those days Jesus went out to a mountainside to pray, and spent the night praying to God. When morning came; he called his disciples to him and chose twelve of them; whom he also designated apostles:

Luke 6:12 – 13 NIV

While I had been arrested in my spirit, it wasn't because Jesus had prayed by Himself because I knew He often prayed by Himself. And it wasn't because He had prayed all night, because again, He often did. Now, I could say that it *was* because *after* He prayed, He received the answer to His prayer, but that would only be half true.

I had been arrested in my spirit because the revelation was *when He prayed, He was under an open heaven!*

As I meditated on this passage of scriptures, I was astonished at the fact that after He had prayed (all night), He got His answer (the next morning)! How do I know He got His answer?

The scripture tells us that when morning came; He called the disciples to Him. He chose the twelve and designated them apostles.

So, there's no doubt in my mind that He was praying about *who He should choose as His twelve disciples. And God revealed to Him who to choose!* He had many disciples! (In Luke, chapter ten, He sent out seventy-two disciples.)

Now let me say this: The thing that was revealed to me was *God was listening!* As Jesus prayed, God was listening! And the vision was before me:

God was sitting on His throne *listening* to Jesus' prayer, then He told Jesus which of the disciples He should choose.

Jesus was sitting under an open heaven!

When Jesus prayed, He had access to God in Heaven!

When all the people were being baptized, Jesus was baptized too. And as he was praying, heaven was opened and the Holy Spirit descended on him in bodily form like a dove. And a voice came from heaven: "You are my Son, whom I love; with you I am well pleased."

Luke 3:21 – 22 NIV (emphasis added)

When we pray, God is listening to us!

When we pray, we are under an open heaven!

When we pray, we have access to God in heaven!

The scripture tells us that *as he was praying the heavens opened.* So apparently, this is not just your "Hi, God. How

[164]

are you?" prayer. At some point during prayer, we have the ability to access God in the heaven. One way to access Him is by praying all night.

And as we pray, heaven will open for us as well. The Holy Spirit will descend; a voice will come from heaven and give us the answer to our prayer.

When we pray, we have access to the Father, the Son, and the Holy Spirit.

Therefore, let us use Jesus' model for answered prayer:

- ✓ He was alone
- ✓ He prayed all night
- ✓ He prayed to God

After He prayed

- ✓ He received the answer

In the morning

- ✓ He called the disciples
- ✓ He chose twelve disciples
- ✓ He appointed them apostles

God is listening to your prayers.

The answer to your prayer is in your all-night prayer.

INCREASE!

And for thy cattle, and for the beast that are in thy land, shall all the increase thereof be meat.

Leviticus 25:7 KJV

GOD WANTS YOU TO REIGN!

Once, having been asked by the Pharisees when the kingdom of God would come, Jesus replied, "The kingdom of God does not come with your careful observation, nor will people say, 'Here it is,' or 'There it is,' because the kingdom of God is within you.

Luke 17:20 – 22 NIV

We're looking for a king. We're looking for a kingdom. We're looking for the place where God rules and reigns.

Where are His power, glory, and authority?

Where is the kingdom of God?

One thing the Lord wants to make clear is His kingdom is not of this world.

The kingdom of God is within us.

This kingdom is a spiritual kingdom.

The *kingdom of God* is a revelation of God coming into the world to demonstrate His glory, power, and authority against the dominion of Satan. It is God expressing Himself with supremacy in all His works. It is an assertion of divine power in action.

[167]

Where is this kingdom?

God's spiritual rule and reign is in the hearts and in the minds of His people. His Holy Spirit dwells in our hearts and our bodies are the temples of the Holy Spirit, which allows His kingdom to be present in the world. He wants to manifest His kingdom; glory, power, and authority in our lives.

He wants to give us spiritual power over Satan's rule.

We are to *preach* the kingdom of God.

We are to *demonstrate* the kingdom of God.

The Great Commission:

He said to them, "Go into all the world and preach the good news to all creation. Whoever believes and is baptized will be saved, but whoever does not believe will be condemned. And these signs will accompany those who believe: In my name they will drive out demons; they will speak in new tongues; they will pick up snakes with their hands; and when they drink deadly poison, it will not hurt them at all; they will place their hands on sick people, and they will get well."

Mark 16:15 – 18 NLT

God has given you the keys to the kingdom and He wants you to reign!

Everything you need to be victorious is ***within*** you. The kingdom of God is ***within*** you.

You have the power and the authority to rule and reign over Satan.

Demonstrate your power.

Demonstrate your authority.

Every time you pray: *your kingdom come, your will be done on earth as it is in heaven* you are praying that *the same realm, the same power, the same authority, the same kingdom of the spirit* that is displayed in heaven would be displayed in you!

You are asking that God would express Himself through you and reveal His glory, assert His authority against the dominion of Satan, and demonstrate His divine powers.

Now take authority!

God wants you to reign!

INCREASE!

For it is the jubilee; it shall be holy unto you: ye shall eat the increase thereof out of the field.

Leviticus 25:12 KJV

MY ALABASTER JAR

With great expectation, I entered the room. Excited about what the Lord was getting ready to do. I knew, without a shadow of a doubt, that He was getting ready to show up with great power. I knew His presence was going to be manifested in great power as His Holy Spirit overshadowed me.

I entered His presence as I had done many times before, filled with expectation and a heart that was excited, and anxious I might add, to see what He was going to do. Never, ever, ever had He let me down before. I came before Him with confidence. I mean, there was no other way for things to turn out; other than how they had turned out all the other times I had come before Him.

However, this time it was different.

There was a slight prompting in my spirit; there was the ever-so-faint presence that something wasn't right. I ignored it. I knew that once I got into His presence, it would go away. But it didn't. In fact, it got worse.

I tried desperately to push past it.

This day, of all days, I needed Him!

I needed Him to do what He said He would do. I needed Him to show me the fruit of my labor. I needed Him to make good on His word; His promise that I had been so diligently waiting on.

In the midst of me stretching my faith, trying to reach out to Him, He revealed Himself to me:

I saw Him on the cross.

The crown of thorns on His head, the nails in His hands and feet, – His blood ran down His bruised and battered body – as He hung on the cross.

But he was wounded for our transgressions, he was bruised for our iniquities: the chastisement of our peace was upon him; and with his stripes we are healed.

Isaiah 53:5 KJV

Disappointment fell on me like a blanket.

I didn't get what I had come expecting; what I was hoping for. And great distress overwhelmed me. So much so, that I had to continue to cry out to Him to, if nothing else, speak to me; speak clear to my heart so that the disappointment would leave. One word from Him and I would be made whole.

The vision spoke volumes: "I did what I said I would do."

And immediately, I had become the woman with the alabaster jar.

While he was eating, a woman came in with a beautiful alabaster jar of expensive perfume made from essence of nard. She broke open the jar and poured the perfume over his head.

Mark 14:3 NLT

As the tears rolled down my face and the need for forgiveness rung out in my spirit, I had become overwhelmed with a heart of repentance. All that I had; my need was in my alabaster jar. I gave it to Him; I poured it out on Him.

Somehow, unlike the many times before, I had lost focus. I had lost sight of Him doing what He said He would do. Somehow, I had lost focus of Him showing me the fruit of my labor. Somehow, I had lost focus of Him making good on His word; His promise that I had been so diligently waiting on.

I continued to weep before Him, asking Him to forgive me.

I, like the woman, had come to Him, broken open my alabaster jar, and gave that which was precious to me, near and dear to my heart – I gave it to Jesus.

Anointing Him with my sorrow.

When we lose sight of Him doing what He said He would do, when we lose sight of Him showing us the fruit of my labor, when we lose sight of Him making good on His word; His promise that we so diligently waiting on, *let us not lose sight of the cross.*

Every promise that He made, He kept.

Everything that we want Him to do, expect Him to do, need Him to do, He has done.

[174]

Let us be mindful to give everything that is near and dear to our hearts to Him; every pain, sorrow, disappointment.

Anoint Him. Bless Him. Give it to Him.

INCREASE!

And if ye shall say, What shall we eat the seventh year? behold, we shall not sow, nor gather in our increase:

Leviticus 25:20 KJV

Week 41
October 7 – October 13

BLESSINGS IN DISGUISE

As I prepare to get in the Lord's presence, the vision is before me:

In a vision...

I saw the ministry increasing.

And immediately, the Lord said, "The more they were oppressed, the more they multiplied."

I was reminded of His word in the book of Exodus:

But the more the Egyptians oppressed them, the more the Israelites multiplied and spread,

Exodus 1:12a NLT

I was excited, I must say, to see the increase in the ministry as the word of the Lord was spoken. But there is nothing more unsettling than hearing the word of the Lord and then seeing something different. So, I have to say, that I was discouraged, to say the least, when there was no increase.

In fact, I had decided that I was throwing in the towel. I was giving up. I was done.

[177]

It seemed as though all of my hard work; my labor; was in vain.

The labor of building the ministry had worn me down. We had in fact, done more at that time than I had ever done; I was making bricks without straw. And just like a Hebrew slave, there was no compensation for my labor.

Burdened, deflated, and defeated at the cost of our labor.

I cried out to the Lord to give me revelation of what was happening; why was it happening? (I often say, "I don't mind going through, as long as I know 'why' I'm going through.") So I needed the Lord to shed some light on what was happening. Why wasn't I seeing any increase in the ministry?

And quick to the draw, the words of encouragement began to come.

And His prompting to "keep going" encouraged me.

When we are burdened, it helps us to go through if we understand that our situation is to make us stronger. When we are discouraged, it helps us go through if we understand that our situations help to develop in us the qualities that will prepare us for the future.

We cannot be overcomers without troubles to overcome.

You have to go through – to get to!

But as long as we stand on God's word, we shall see the promises of God manifest in our lives. I have His word: the ministry increasing. "The more we're oppressed, the more we'll multiply." (The more we go through, the more we'll be victorious in overcoming.)

It was during the most difficult times of our ministry, when we continued to press, that we experienced the greatest blessings.

Our burdens, trials, tests are usually God's blessings in disguise.

Remain faithful to God in the hard times, the difficult times, the times of uncertainty because He's preparing you to receive the blessings!

INCREASE!

Thou shalt truly tithe all the increase of thy seed, that the field bringeth forth year by year.

Deuteronomy 14:22 KJV

EXPECT THE UNEXPECTED

The Lord said, "Expect the unexpected."

Immediately, I knew in my spirit, the Lord is getting ready to do the unexpected.

As He made His plan known, He also made known there is no way that we can prepare for the blessings that He has in store for us.

The plans that we have, however grand, limits God!

Don't try to figure it out. Don't try to plan it to the "T."

There has to be room for God to do the miraculous.

Expect the unexpected!

I can't begin to tell you how excited I've been these last few months in expectation of what the Lord is getting ready to do. I mean, the excitement has mounted so much so that I don't think I'm any different than the kids at Christmas. I'm in expectation of the blessings that I'm getting ready to receive from the Lord.

And *whatever* it is, *whatever* they are, I know it's just for me!

I mean, I'm sooo excited I'm about to burst. I'm almost at a point that I cannot hold it in any longer. And the closer I get, the more the excitement builds. There would be no need for an introduction, you don't have to tell me where to look, when I see it, I'll know that's it!

I'm ready to receive the blessings!

We have to take the limits off of what God is doing in this hour.

We have to expect the unexpected.

After we've done all that we can do, say, "Okay, Lord, now put your super on my natural!" And watch Him do the impossible. What you thought couldn't be done, God's getting ready to do it! It's going to be huge! God is getting ready to blow your mind!

Now unto Him that is able to do exceeding abundantly above all that we ask or think, according to the power that worketh in us.

Ephesians 3:20 KJV

There are no limits with God.

Your age doesn't matter. Your color doesn't matter. Your size doesn't matter. Your education doesn't matter. Your job doesn't matter. Your house doesn't matter. Your car doesn't matter. Your money doesn't matter.

God is getting ready to do the miraculous!

I mean, I'm so filled with expectation that everything that's within me cries out with the anticipation. As in childbirth,

[182]

I'm expecting the manifestation of what God is getting ready to do. Right now!

I'm ready, God!

Take the limits off!

Expect the unexpected!

And receive the manifested blessings of the Lord!

INCREASE!

---

*Seven days shalt thou keep a solemn feast unto
the LORD thy God in the place which the LORD shall
choose: because the LORD thy God shall bless thee in all
thine increase, and in all the works of thine hands,
therefore thou shalt surely rejoice.*

Deuteronomy 16:15 KJV

Week 43
October 21 – October 27

BREAK FREE

Every day was a challenge that got more and more difficult to face as the days went by. The Lord continued to call me, but I couldn't bring myself to go to Him; one day after the other; then another, and still yet another.

After several days, I realized that my reluctance was more than "I don't feel like it."

Each day I would make plans and encourage myself that no matter what I would go to Him in the morning. However, each morning was met with the same reluctance, fear. And somehow I'd tell myself that tomorrow would be different. Tomorrow would be the day that I'd throw off all restraints and go to Him.

But tomorrow never came.

I continued to struggle to get in His presence. I continued to struggle with what He was telling me to do. I had struggled to even accomplish what I had accomplished, and it was clear that I wasn't sure if I was going to be able to complete it all.

My heart's desire was to do all that He had called me to do, but even my desire wasn't enough to get it done. I knew what great accomplishment it would be to get it done, and still I couldn't seem to get it done. Somehow the fear was too great.

My hands had become heavy; I was unable to do the work that the Lord had called me to do. I kept thinking about the many mistakes that I had made. The fear of my mistakes was overwhelming. I kept going over it and over it, again and again and again. Every time I thought about it, I wanted desperately to change it. Then I finally convinced myself to just step back, so that I could clear my mind.

I was afraid.

One thing I realized was the fact that I wasn't going to be able to get it done by myself. I continued to ask the Lord to help me push pass the fear, so that I could finish what He had told me to do.

I kept going over it again and again and again, but still couldn't seem to get it accomplished.

I shared with my husband that I was struggling with the *spirit of fear.* And I shared how difficult the challenge had become. I wasn't able to move forward.

As my husband prayed for me, he began declaring the word of the Lord and suddenly, my hands broke free! Immediately, I felt the weight lift from my hands; the chains that were holding me back had been broken! My hands were free to finish the work that the Lord had given me.

And when the chains had been broken, I was able to release it into the Lord's hands. I was able to let go and allow the Lord to do in me, with me as He saw fit. I was able to see clearly what I believe was what He wanted me to do.

I released it!

I was free.

And as I continued to do the work, it was easy.

What challenges are you faced with? What difficulties? What's hold you back from doing what the Lord has called you to do?

Have you tried time and time again to push through it, but can't? Have you tried to break free to no avail? Sometimes, we have to share our burdens so that we can get the help that we need.

Break free!

INCREASE!

And sow the fields, and plant vineyards, which may yield fruits of increase.

Psalm 107:37 KJV

REMAIN FAITHFUL

The Lord keeps reminding me of the widow woman with the two mites. And little by little, as He ministers to me, I get the revelation:

He sees my sacrifice.

The Lord is very much aware of everything that's going on with us. There is nothing that we're going through that He's not aware of.

Something in you encourages you to continue to be faithful even though you don't see anything happening. You continue to pray, but your prayers go unanswered. You continue to read His word; stand on His word, and still nothing happens. You continue to go to the House of the Lord, and seemingly He's not there. You continue to minister to others, and yet, no one ministers to you. You continue to do the work of the Lord, but no one supports your ministry.

In spite of everything, you've remained faithful.

Therefore, I want to share with you, ***He sees your sacrifice.***

Every time you're faithful even though you don't see anything happening. Every time you pray, but your prayers go unanswered. Every time you read His word; stand on His word, and still nothing happens. Every time you go to the House of the Lord, and seemingly He's not there. Every time you minister to others, and yet, no one ministers to you. Every time you do the work of the Lord, but no one supports your ministry…*He sees your sacrifice.*

And as long as you remain faithful, He's going to reward your faithfulness.

Don't' think for a moment that God is going to allow you to continue to make sacrifices for Him – and He not reward you.

Rest assured that He sees what you're doing. He sees what you're going through, and in due season, He's going to reward your faithfulness.

Be encouraged.

Don't grow weary in well doing. You will reap the harvest if you faint not.

I know it can be discouraging sometimes, but now is not the time to give up. Now is not the time to draw back. Now is not the time to give in. Now is not the time to slack off.

You are closer now to receiving the blessing than you've ever been.

Remain faithful.

Keep doing what you've been doing because God is going to reward your faithfulness.

[190]

Keep being faithful even though you don't see anything happening. Keep praying even though your prayers seem to go unanswered. Keep reading His word; standing on His word even though nothing seems to happen. Keep going to the House of the Lord even though seemingly He's not there. Keep ministering to others even though no one's ministering to you. Keep doing the work of the Lord even though no one supports your ministry because God is going to reward your faithfulness.

God is going to reward your diligence.

God is going to reward your stewardship.

God is going to reward you for all of the sacrifices that you've made.

Be encouraged.

He's going to reward you, soon.

INCREASE!

Wealth gotten by vanity shall be diminished: but he that gathereth by labour shall increase.

Proverbs 13:11 KJV

GO BACK SEVEN TIMES

I'm reminded of a time when I was first getting to know God. I wanted more of Him. I don't necessarily think I was desperate for Him, but I was excited about our "new" relationship and wanted more.

I wanted to learn more in order to get to know Him.

I remember I would listen to the Sunday sermon every day for a week; seven days, in order to try to get to know Him more; in order to learn more about Him; in order to learn more about our new relationship; in order to know what was going on in my life.

I made it a habit to listen to the sermon every day, for one hour, while I did my workout. So there were no distractions; just me and God, focused. Not that I looked forward to the workouts, but I looked forward to hearing the message. Immediately, I started to realize that as I listened to the sermon, I had heard something in the sermon *that* day that I hadn't heard the day before. And needless to say, I was excited.

The next day I listened to the sermon, and again, I heard something *that* day that I hadn't heard the day before.

And more and more, I got excited because I was seeing God in a way that I had never seen Him before. He had

[193]

ministered to me in a way that He hadn't ministered before, which kept me coming back for more. I looked forward to it.

It was all that I wanted to do; to learn more, to get to know Him more.

And every time I listened to the sermon, there was something that I hadn't heard before.

Now, I can't help but be reminded of Naaman, and his desire to be healed of leprosy. The prophet Elisha told him to go and dip seven times in the river Jordan and he would be healed.

Elisha sent a messenger to say to him, "Go, wash yourself seven times in the Jordan, and your flesh will be restored and you will be cleansed."

So he went down and dipped himself in the Jordan seven times, as the man of God had told him, and his flesh was restored and became clean like that of a young boy.

2 Kings 5:10, 14 NIV

As I was preparing for this writing, I kept hearing the Lord say, "Go back seven times."

In order for us to receive what God has for us, we have do what He tells us to do; we have to meditate on His word. We have to allow Him to minister to us through His word. How many times have we **heard** the word of God and never got anything out of it? How many times have we **read** the word of God and didn't get anything out of it? Somehow, we thought, the word wasn't for us?

God has a word for you, but you have to be obedient to His command in order to receive it.

God's word doesn't return to Him void. It accomplishes what He sent it out to accomplish. I don't think it's possible that you can hear the word of God and it not prosper (if anything, it may not be *the season),* but if you hear the word of the Lord it is for you. However, I also believe and understand we don't receive the word because we don't take the time to meditate on the word. Thereby, we forfeit the blessing.

Apparently, it's not enough to just hear the word once. We have to continuously hear the word until it takes root in our spirit. It is our responsibility to meditate on the word in order to become proficient in the things of God.

The word is our daily bread.

This book of the law shall not depart out of thy mouth; but thou shalt meditate therein day and night, that thou mayest observe to do according to all that is written therein: for then thou shalt make thy way prosperous, and then thou shalt have good success.

Joshua 1:8 KJV

We need to know what God is saying to us daily. Every day He has something to say to us. And on *that* day He will make His word known to you.

He'll give you a little bit at a time; He won't overwhelm you. So every day, for seven days, meditate on the word of God. The same word, and watch Him show you things that you'd never seen before. Watch Him tell you things that you'd never heard before.

Do what He says.

Seven is the number of completion.

And like Naaman, whatever you're dealing with – you won't have to deal with it anymore!

INCREASE!

Where no oxen are, the crib is clean: but much increase is by the strength of the ox.

Proverbs 14:4 KJV

Week 46
November 11 – November 17

THE SEASON HAS CHANGED

I found myself in unfamiliar territory. What I thought was a call to pray was not prayer as I had known it. And in the midst of me searching and looking for Jesus, I found myself getting a little anxious and irritated.

I had come for prayer.

I kept looking at my watch, wanting it to be over; I wanted to leave. But, strange enough, for some reason I couldn't leave. There seemed to be a little prompting in my spirit, a little bit of hope that the prayer would happen. I was expecting prayer. And subconsciously, I wasn't leaving until there was prayer.

During the first hour, I understood that it was time dedicated to just me and God. Honor Him any way that I pleased. If I wanted to pray, pray. If I wanted to sing, sing. If I wanted to dance, dance. If I wanted to worship, worship. Whatever my heart desired I could do. I sat there taking mental notes. I looked around to see what was happening (even though the lights were out and only pot lights lit the room – just enough to know there were people in the room).

The atmosphere challenged my expectations.

[198]

And while I was going to allow things to run their course, I gave in to the temptation of knowing if there was going to be prayer, at some point. So I asked.

There would be prayer.

But as the time passed, seemingly, *that night* wasn't going to be the night that the prayer was going to happen.

Finally, I saw someone go onto the platform. Immediately, I got excited in my spirit. It was time for prayer. An invitation for me to come down to the altar to worship the Lord was extended. I stood on my feet (in anticipation and in agreement with the prayer that was getting ready to go forth).

Again, an invitation for me to come down to the altar to worship the Lord was extended.

So I continued to worship the Lord.

There would be no prayer I reasoned.

Then from out of nowhere, someone started praying, fervently and with vigor. As if they had been praying for a long time they went in hard; with energy and force; passionately. As I stood in agreement, I have to say, it wasn't prayer like I knew prayer.

I wasn't really sure of what was happening, but I stood in agreement with the word of God.

I settled within myself that it was all about worship. It wasn't prayer, but rather worship.

I left the place disappointed, unfortunately, because of my expectations.

The next morning I knew something happened in the spirit as a result of me being in that atmosphere. I wasn't sure of what, but I knew something happened, which became apparent in my prayer.

For a season I couldn't pray; I could only worship the Lord. Although I wanted to pray, when I tried to pray, I couldn't; I could only worship. Then suddenly, I realized a shift had taken place in the spirit.

The season had changed.

The worship atmosphere was conducive to the shift.

I had been ushered into a new season.

A *spirit of worship* had been birth forth.

I was in a place of peace.

And as I thought about all that was going on in my life, the Lord's peace rested upon me. You see, there comes a time when you've done all that you can do, you cried and prayed; you prayed and cried, and there isn't anything else that you can do, *not even pray.*

Sometimes all you have to do is worship the Lord.

The season has changed.

...Thus saith the LORD unto you, Be not afraid nor dismayed by reason of this great multitude; for the battle is not yours, but God's.

2 Chronicles 20:15 KJV

INCREASE!

When the wicked rise, men hide themselves: but when they perish, the righteous increase.

Proverbs 28:28 KJV

YOU DON'T HAVE TO WORRY

I know I don't have to tell you this because you probably already know, but I'm going to tell you anyway.

It's not easy to keep your eyes on Jesus.

I don't care how much you pray. I don't care how much you speak in tongues. I don't care how much you worship. I don't care how much you read the bible; it's not easy to keep your eyes on Jesus.

And it's difficult to wait on the promise. It's difficult to wait for your "due season." It's difficult to *not* grow weary in well doing.

It's difficult.

And it's that much more difficult when you see everyone else around you getting blessed. Everyone else around you has come into their "due season." Everyone else around you is progressing, while you're still waiting.

You can't help but wonder *when is my turn? How much longer do I have to wait?*

Better yet, *why am I waiting?* you wonder.

I mean, everywhere you look, it's something! You're struggling with your job, but your friend just got promoted. You're struggling to make ends meet, but your friend is just "blowing" money. You're barely making it in the car you have, but your friend just got a new car. You're struggling to pay your rent, but your friend just bought a new house. You're struggling to get your ministry started, but your friend's ministry is growing.

I mean, it's one thing after another!

However, at some point, you're going to have to make a conscious decision that it doesn't matter what is going on around you, it doesn't matter what is going on with everybody else, you're going to wait on God! At some point, you're going to have to resolve that you're going to rejoice with your friend who got the promotion; you're going to rejoice with the friend who's not suffering financially; you're going to rejoice with the friend who got the new car; you're going to rejoice with the friend who bought the new house; you're going to rejoice with the friend who's doing the work of the Lord, and you're going to keep your eyes on Jesus.
Amen?!

So many times we fail to realize that what the Lord is doing *in us* is *not* what He's doing in everybody else. Wait! Let me say it this way: we fail to realize that what the Lord is doing *in everybody else* is *not* what He's doing in us. And we have to *know that we know that we know* God has great things in store for us. And whenever He sees fit to release the blessings, it's going to be huge!

So often we're so focused on what's *not* happening for us that we fail to see what *is* happening for us.

God is doing something in your life that you have to be thankful for.

It may not be the new job, the new car, the new house, the growing ministry, but it's something! God is doing *something* in your life! And if you'll focus on *that* – if you'll focus on what He *is* doing in your life and thank Him for *that,* you'll see you're just as blessed as "everybody" else.

When we take our eyes off of the Lord, that's when we start to doubt Him. That's when we start wondering *"if"* it's going to happen, *"when"* it's going to happen, *"how"* it's going to happen. There's no need for you to *try* to figure out what God is doing. Just do what He told you to do, and He'll take care of the rest.

Don't stop doing what you're doing.

He hasn't forgotten about you. He sees you. He knows exactly what's going on.

And when you get into a place where you **trust** Him, He'll begin to show up and show out for you.

But you have to put your trust in *Him.*

The Lord said, "You don't have to worry."

He's going to take care of everything; every promise will come to pass.

Here's the key: What He's doing in you, through you, for you, to you, is *not* what He's doing in, through, for, or to anybody else.

Your blessings are tailor-made.

They are designed to fit you, exclusively.

DON'T WORRY. YOUR BLESSING IS ON THE WAY!

INCREASE!

Of the increase of his government and peace there shall be no end, upon the throne of David, and upon his kingdom, to order it, and to establish it with judgment and with justice from henceforth even for ever. The zeal of the LORD *of hosts will perform this.*

Isaiah 9:7 KJV

PRAISE HIM!

We are creatures of habit: Day in and day out, doing the same things over and over; set in our ways. But then one day, out of nowhere something happens; there's an interruption in our daily routine. We can't seem to move forward; can't seem to pull it together.

We're going about our daily routine and can't seem to make it happen. Nothing is working out. And nobody has the answer.

God is trying to get our attention.

Sometimes, God will interrupt our daily schedule; stop us from doing anything else to get us to praise Him!

And our only option is to seek His face; the face of Him who is the only One who can make it right, and put us on the right path.

During this Thanksgiving holiday, let's not forget to give Him the praise.

Praise Him!

Get in His presence and give Him some praise!

God wants us to praise Him. Not for a breakthrough. Not for a blessing.

Praise Him because of who He is!

He's our Lord and Savior, Bright and Morning Star, Prince of Peace, Everlasting Father. He's the King of kings; the Lord of Lords, our Sovereign God; our Holy and Righteous God, the Creator of heaven and earth. Our Protector, Provider, Strong tower that we run to and are safe. Our Deliverer; the Lover of our souls!

Hallelujah!

He sits on the throne with all power and authority in His hands. He sits high, but He looks low and watches closely what goes on in the earth. There is nothing that can happen without His permission!

Hallelujah!

Praise Him!

Let everything that has breath praise the Lord!

PRAISE YE the Lord.
Praise God in his sanctuary:
praise him in the firmament of his power.
Praise him for his mighty acts: praise him according to his excellent greatness.
Praise him with the sound of the trumpet: praise him with the psaltery and harp.
Praise him with the timbrel and dance: praise him with stringed instruments and organs.
Praise him upon the loud cymbals: praise him upon the high sounding cymbals.

Let every thing that hath breath praise the LORD. Praise ye the LORD.

Psalm 150:1-6 KJV

INCREASE!

Then shall he give the rain of thy seed, that thou shalt sow the ground withal; and bread of the increase of the earth, and it shall be fat and plenteous: in that day shall thy cattle feed in large pastures.

Isaiah 30:23 KJV

WORSHIP HIM

Sometimes we find ourselves in that difficult position of not hearing from the Lord, seeing Him, or getting the blessings we're looking for.

And it's difficult to stay in that place as we become anxious, and sometimes even weary, as we wait on the Lord.

The frustration mounts. The pressure to do something mounts. The anxiety, worry, doubt, confusion mounts as we continue to wait.

If only we can hear a word from Him, we'd be strengthened. We'd be able to stand. We'd be able to take that next step. We'd be able to go that extra mile. We'd be able to hold on.

But seemingly, we've done all that we can. We've done all that we know to do.

We cried and prayed. We prayed and cried. We fasted. We sought godly counsel.

We sought the Lord.

And still, there's no answer.

The call seems to go unanswered.

When you've done all that you know to do, worship Him.

You have to find Him in a place of peace. You have to remove all the frustration, the pressure to do something, the anxiety, worry, doubt, confusion, and fear.

Then you'll find Him in the peace.

Just worship Him until you find Him.

Worship Him until you hear that small still voice.

"Go out and stand before me on the mountain,"
the LORD told him. And as Elijah stood there,
the LORD passed by, and a mighty windstorm hit the
mountain. It was such a terrible blast that the rocks were
torn loose, but the LORD was not in the wind. After the
wind there was an earthquake, but the LORD was not in
the earthquake. And after the earthquake there was a
fire, but the LORD was not in the fire. And after the fire
there was the sound of a gentle whisper. When Elijah
heard it, he wrapped his face in his cloak and went out
and stood at the entrance of the cave.

And a voice said, "What are you doing here, Elijah?"

1 Kings 19 11-13 NLT

Just like you won't find Him in the wind, you won't find Him in the frustration or in the pressure to do something. Just like you won't find Him in the earthquake, you won't find Him in the anxiety, worry, doubt or confusion. And just like you won't find Him in the fire, you won't find Him in the fear.

But you *will* find Him in worship.

You *will* find Him in that gentle whisper.

And He'll speak to your frustration. He'll speak to the pressure to do something. He'll speak to the anxiety, worry, doubt, confusion. And He'll speak to the fear.

When we've done all that we can do, worship Him!

All you need to do is find Him.

And He'll answer.

Worship Him.

INCREASE!

Israel was holiness unto the LORD, and the firstfruits of his increase: all that devour him shall offend; evil shall come upon them, saith the LORD.

Jeremiah 2:3 KJV

ACCORDING TO YOUR ABILITY

God has entrusted something into your hands and He is not only expecting you to work it, He is expecting it to increase!

When I look around at what He's given me, and the many opportunities I have for them to grow, I understand the importance of the process. I understand that I'm not able to do what *I* want to do because I haven't been prepared for what I want to do. I haven't gone through the process of doing what He has given me to do.

Here's a revelation: Doing what He has given me to do is going to prepare me to do what it is that I want to do.

Yes, it's a part of the blessing that God has for me, but I have to be prepared for it.

God wants to see what you're going to do with what he has given you.

Let's take a look:

To one he gave five bags of gold, to another two bags, and to another one bag, <u>each according to his ability.</u>

> ***Matthew 25:15 NIV (emphasis added)***

Not only has God entrusted us with doing the work, but the measure in which He has given us is according to each of our own ability. In other words, it doesn't matter what He gave to someone else, and it doesn't matter how well someone else does it. What matters is what He gave you, what he gave me, and how well *we're* able to get it done.

He gives according to our ability.

He gives according to what we're capable of doing. He doesn't give to us based on someone else's ability. He doesn't give to us based on what someone else is capable of doing.

What you have is based on what you are capable of handling. And He expects it to increase.

He gave to one five bags because that's what he was capable of handling. He didn't give everybody five bags because everybody isn't capable of handling five bags. That's why he gave to one two bags and the other one bag. He knows what we're capable of.

It doesn't matter the amount that you've received, He expects an increase.

The man who had received five bags of silver went at once and put his money to work and gained five bags more. So also, the one with two bags of silver gained two more. But the man who received the one bag of silver dug a hole in the ground and hid his master's money.

Matthew 25:16 – 18 NLT

What are you doing with what God has given you?

Sometimes we're so focused on getting to the next level or getting to the "blessing" that we're not focused on doing what God has given us to do. We're missing the blessing of what *we* have. We're missing the blessing of what God has given *us* to do.

Let us be faithful with that which the Lord has given us.

To the man who had received five bags and the man who had received two bags:

"The master said, 'Well done, my good and faithful servant. You have been faithful in handling this small amount, so now I will give you many more responsibilities. Let's celebrate together!'

To the man who had received one bag*:*

"Then he ordered, 'Take the money from this servant, and give it to the one with the ten bags of silver. To those who use well what they are given, even more will be given, and they will have an abundance. <u>But from those who do nothing, even what little they have will be taken away.</u>
Matthew 25:23; 28 – 29 NLT (emphasis added)

To whom much is given, much is required.

- ✓ What you do with what God has given you will determine if you will get more.
- ✓ What you do with what God has given you will determine if you will get the "blessing."
- ✓ What you do with what God has given you will determine if what you've been given will be taken away, and given to someone else.

Therefore, let us be mindful to work that which the Lord has given us; that it may increase, and that we may receive more.

Use what you have to the glory of God.

INCREASE!

I will also save you from all your uncleannesses: and I will call for the corn, and will increase it, and lay no famine upon you.

Ezekiel 36:29 KJV

NOW FAITH

I think it goes without saying that Hebrews 11:1 is a very familiar passage of scripture:

Now faith is <u>the substance of things hoped for</u>, the evidence of things not seen.

Hebrews 11:1 KJV (emphasis added)

In fact, it's so familiar that I don't think there is anything anyone else can say about this passage of scripture that hasn't already been said. Well, man can't say anything else about it, however, God, on the other hand can.

It's unfortunate, but so very often we miss out on what God is doing in our lives or we miss out on the blessings because we don't receive it by faith. Often times it really just comes down to us *believing* that God said we can do what He says we can do and we can have what He says we can have. It's that simple, right?

Right.

But for many of us, it's not that simple. Why isn't it?

Because we don't *walk* by faith; we don't *live* by faith. Instead, we *walk* by sight; we *live* by time and resources.

Faith is not subject to time. Faith is not subject to resources.

NOW IS FAITH – FAITH IS NOW!

Now means at the present time. It doesn't mean "in the past" and it doesn't mean "in the future." It means, "now."

However, the issue that we have with faith, often times, is that we don't operate in the NOW. We don't operate by faith. We operate in time and by resources.

Again, faith is not subject to time. Faith is not subject to resources.

We are **subject to,** we are **bound by,** we are **limited by,** and we are **under the authority of** resources and time.

We are subject to "when the time is right." We are bound by "when I get the money." We are bound by "when I get the resources." We are under the authority of "wait!"
So we wait.

We wait for the time. We wait for the people. We wait for the money. We wait for the resources. We wait for the job. We wait for the house. We wait for the car. We wait for the degrees.

Then we miss the blessing!

Let us remove the restraints that so easily beset us. Let us take off the limits, so that we may *walk* by faith, *live* by faith, and accomplish the things that God has for us to accomplish. Let us receive the blessings that God has in store for us.

[222]

Let's take that step of faith.

Take the limits off. Come from under the authority of 'whatever' is keeping you from moving forward in the things of God.

We are not **subject** to anything.

We are not **bound** by anything.

We are not **limited** by anything.

We are not **under the rule of anything or anyone.**

But God.

Take the limits off.

Let God be God.

Allow Him to bless you, NOW.

Today, make the decision to *walk* by faith, *live* by faith. Whenever the Lord tells you to do something, do it! Don't limit *Him* because you don't have the time or resources that you think you need.

All you need is faith.

When you have faith ***that's*** NOW.

When you have "the present time," that's when you act.

The Lord is saying, "Do it NOW!"

INCREASE!

But Saul increased the more in strength, and confounded the Jews which dwelt at Damascus, proving that this is very Christ.

Acts 9:22 KJV

TAKE THE LIMITS OFF!

Here it is, two days after our first TOYS FOR CHRISTMAS toy giveaway and I'm still thinking about how awesome it was, and how amazing God is for all He has done to make this happen.

I can't even begin to tell you how awesome it was pulling it all together. From the five, maybe six, hours of shopping for the toys, taking inventory of everything we had (making sure we had enough), to decorating the Christmas tree in preparation for all the kids we were expecting to show up.

While doing so, old memories of my husband and I getting ready for Santa started to surface as I prepared the toys and "gift wrapped" the boxes; memories of our own kids and how excited they would be when they saw the toys and eagerly grabbed for the first "big" thing that caught their eye. Excitement filled the room as if I was getting ready for Santa like the days of old.

On the day of the toy drive, the excitement only seemed to build. I couldn't wait for the children to come and get the toys. How excited they were going to be. I knew that already. I could just imagine the excitement in anticipation of what toys they would end up with.

Surely, they would come with expectation of what toys would be there; expectation of the toys that they wanted

Santa to bring. And my only hope was that the toys that they wanted would be the toys that they found under the tree.

To be honest, I don't know who was more excited them or me.

The tree, donated as well, brand new, and complete with lights and ornaments, stood over six feet tall and towered over the toys and sparkled with Christmas magic with a star as its crown.

We knew the children weren't coming for the tree. They were coming for the toys that were under the tree. My only hope was that the tree would prove its strength to stand, once the kids started searching for the toys that would undoubtedly be buried beneath all the other toys.

And then they came.

The kids had arrived.

And one by one, the smiles on their wide-eyed faces quickly turned into excitement the very moment they saw the toys. Not even acknowledging me as I stood to welcome them, they ran right to the toys and started searching for "the" toys that they would choose.

I tried to help guide them to where they would find the toys that they may have been looking for. I asked how old they were, and with each response I showed them the area in which they would find toys that were appropriate for their ages.

Well, at least it started out that way, but quickly ended up with them just getting whatever toys they wanted and I have no idea if they were "age appropriate" or not. All I know was they had gotten the toys that "they" wanted.

Then, there was the added assistance from the parents; helping the younger children decide which toys to choose making the moment that much more memorable. And in the midst of all the excitement, we were trying to take pictures to try to capture the moment.

And at one point, there were so many kids that I seemed to have gotten lost in the midst. Turning here, pointing over there, and somehow, I lost sight of the "set up" that I had established of how I was "handling" everything.

Then from out of nowhere, someone tapped me on the shoulder. I turned around to a girl asking me, in a voice of uncertainty, if she could have the "make your own glow in the dark bracelets." To which I answered excitedly, "Sure!" Then, in my attempt to help her find other toys that she may like, I asked her, "How old are you?"

"Thirteen," she responded enthusiastically. Then she walked away as if she had found the *one* thing that she had been looking for. And in the midst of all that was going on, she disappeared just as suddenly as she had appeared.

That moment, I have to say, is one of my highlight moments for a couple of reasons.

One, as I mentioned above, because of how excited she was. It somehow seemed to be a different type of excitement than the other kids as they searched through the toys. This excitement indicated that this gift meant something on the inside. And all of a sudden, none of the other toys seemed to matter. She had found what she was looking for. There was something about that gift that made her choose it.

What? I will probably never know.

The other reason that this was a highlight moment for me is the fact that as we prepared for this toy giveaway, we specifically had children ages up to ten-years old in mind. But to see that a thirteen year old had come, expecting to receive, did my heart good. Not only had she come, but there was something there for her.

There was something there for her. God made sure there was something there for her.

I was in awe.

There was something about *that* moment that seemed to ring out in my spirit.

While in the Lord's presence, I couldn't help but to continue to think about the moment and how excited I was that she came; and being reminded of what the gift could've possibly meant to her. *This* was the very reason we had the toy giveaway.

Then the Lord started to minister to me.

He quickly pointed out the fact that we had prepared for kids up to ten-years old; we were "expecting" kids up to ten-years old.

Then He said, "Take the limits off."

And immediately, the tears rolled down my face and my heart started to break at the thought that we had somehow excluded someone.

But this little girl had somehow dared to come anyway, even though we weren't "expecting" her.

It's sad to say that the same holds true with our expectations of Jesus.

How many times has He tried to bless us with "more than enough" and our expectations limited Him to "what we thought was appropriate"?

Let's take the limits off of what God can do!

Let's make room for Him to perform miracles!

Let's allow Him to go above and beyond what we can ask or think!

Let's believe that He can make ways out of no ways!

Let's expect Him to create doors where there are no doors!

Let's anticipate Him doing the impossible!

Let's expect the unexpected!

Take the limits off!

INCREASE!

He giveth power to the faint; and to them that have no might he increaseth strength.

Isaiah 40:29 KJV

ABOUT DAISY S. DANIELS

Daisy S. Daniels has been married to Randolph E. Daniels, Sr. for 23 years. They have three children: Ronald, DaiSha, and Randolph, Jr. Daisy is Pastor of The Embassy of Grace (co-laborer with Senior Pastor, Randolph Daniels). She is an anointed woman of God who operates in the apostolic five-fold ministry in the body of Christ; under a prophetic mantle.

Prophetess Daisy's leadership, motivational, and transformational expertise encourages, inspires, and empowers the body of Christ.

She is founder and CEO of Daisy S. Daniels Ministries; a ministry that empowers women to increase in mind, body, soul and spirit; to break spiritual, physical, psychological, emotional, and sexual strongholds.

She is President and CEO of The Writing on the Wall Publishing Services; a full-service Christian publishing house that is committed to excellence in Christian-theme publications that enables you to write and publish the books of your dreams.

She received her M.B.A. in International Business from Keller Graduate School of Management in 2011.

TO CONTACT THE AUTHOR

Write: Daisy S. Daniels
P.O. BOX 621194
Orlando, FL 32862
Telephone: (708) 704-6117
Email: daisysdaniels@aol.com
Website: www.daisysdaniels.wix.com/ministry

ALSO BY DAISY S. DANIELS

THE TIES THAT BIND

BREAD FROM HEAVEN

BIRTHING MINISTRY

21-DAY FAITH FAST

YOUR FAITH IS ON TRIAL

THE WRITING ON THE WALL
PUBLISHING SERVICES

The Writing on the Wall Publishing Services is a Christian publishing house that is committed to excellence in Christian-theme publications.

The Writing on the Wall Publishing Services' goal is to equip you with the tools needed to successfully write, publish, and print your intellectual property, which will allow you to minister to the nations and advance the Kingdom of God. Our services include:

- MANUSCRIPT REVIEW
- EDITING
- MANUSCRIPT DEVELOPMENT / CONSULTING
- PAGE DESIGN AND LAYOUT
- COVER DESIGN
- ISBN NUMBER / BOOKLAND EAN BARCODE
- PRINTING
- COPYRIGHT

For more information, contact us:

Write: The Writing on the Wall Publishing Services
P.O. BOX 621433
Orlando, FL 32862 – 1433
Telephone: (708) 704-6117
Website: www.thewritingonthewal.wix.com/daisysdaniels
Email: thewritingonthewall@aol.com

[234]